IN SEARCH OF SOUTH AMERICA

IN SEARCH
OF
SOUTH AMERICA

Reader's Digest

PUBLISHED BY THE READER'S DIGEST ASSOCIATION LIMITED
LONDON   NEW YORK   MONTREAL   SYDNEY   CAPE TOWN

Originally published in partwork form,
Des Pays et des Hommes,
by Librairie Larousse, Paris

A Reader's Digest selection

IN SEARCH OF SOUTH AMERICA

First English Edition Copyright © 1993
The Reader's Digest Association Limited, Berkeley Square House,
Berkeley Square, London W1X 6AB

Copyright © 1993
Reader's Digest Association Far East Limited
Philippines Copyright 1993
Reader's Digest Association Far East Limited

Originally published in French as a partwork,
Des Pays et des Hommes
Copyright © 1991
Librairie Larousse

Translated and edited by Toucan Books Limited, London
Translated and adapted by J. Anderson Black

ISBN 0 276 42056 X

Printed by Printer Industria Gráfica S.A., Barcelona

Contents

COVER PICTURES

Top: *The ruins of the Inca city of Machu Picchu in the Peruvian Andes.*
The city, one of the last strongholds of the Incas before they were destroyed by the Spanish,
lay undiscovered until 1911.
Bottom: *A young Aymara Indian with her baby in the Bolivian Andes.*
More than half the population of Bolivia is of pure Indian stock.

Andean Realms where the Lord Inca Ruled

'The range of mountains called the Andes is accounted one of the greatest in the world,' wrote the 16th-century Spanish chronicler of the Americas, Pedro Cieza de León. It 'is known to begin at the Straits of Magellan [near South America's southern tip] and stretches right through this kingdom of Peru, traversing innumerable lands and provinces. It contains great numbers of high mountains, some of them covered with snow and others belching fire.'

South America's great mountain chain is indeed an imposing barrier. From the Caribbean shore of Venezuela in the north, it runs like a knotted spine down the entire length of the continent's western edge, through the successive republics of Colombia, Ecuador, Peru, Bolivia and Chile, until it dies finally in the near-Antarctic wastes of Tierra del Fuego. In all, it stretches over 5000 miles from north to south, though it is never more than 400 miles wide. It contains numerous volcanoes – including Mount Cotopaxi in Ecuador, at 19,344 feet above sea level the world's highest active volcano – and forms part of the Pacific Ocean's great 'Ring of Fire'. Created by the collision of the so-called Nazca Plate of the eastern Pacific with the South American continent, it is inevitably subject to violent and destructive earthquakes. Several peaks, such as Huascaran in Peru, rise over 22,000 feet, so that the Andes rank second only to the Himalayas for average height.

The Andes' peoples, and their histories and cultures, are as varied and dramatic as its landscapes. Long before any European set foot in the Americas, the central Andes had nurtured a succession of impressive civilisations, culminating in the minutely ordered glories of the Inca empire. Then came the shock of the new in the shape of the intrepid, though unscrupulous, Spanish *conquistador* Francisco Pizarro and a band of 179 followers who landed in the north of modern Peru in 1532. Confronted with the alarming novelties of cannons, horse-mounted soldiers and, in the long term, a more deadly weapon, European diseases to which the native South American peoples had no in-built resistance, the Inca empire tumbled with astonishing rapidity. Spanish rule then flourished for nearly 300 years, until it too fell victim – this time to the nationalist aspirations of the new South Americans. In the first decades of the 19th century, the 'Great Liberator' Simón Bolívar in the north, the Argentinian-born José de San Martín in the south and Chile's half-Irish liberator Bernardo O'Higgins led successful independence struggles – with judicious aid from Britain, happy to see the discomfiture of an empire that rivalled its own.

Out of these events, new societies and new countries were born. Most of them have remained dogged by instability – coups and counter-coups, guerrilla insurgencies and, most recently, the deadly, multi-million-dollar activities of drugs traffickers, all feeding off glaring inequalities of wealth and poverty. But, for all that, the Andean republics remain places of enormous, if sometimes dangerous, appeal and fascination. The melting pot of the centuries has left them with an extraordinary range of peoples and cultures: Indian peoples living much as their ancestors have done for thousands of years in the still dense jungles of the Amazon basin, running off the Andes' eastern flanks; the Indians of the high plateaus, still speaking the Quechua language of the Incas or the even older Aymara tongue, and still practising religious rites rooted in their Inca and pre-Inca past, despite a veneer of Roman Catholic orthodoxy; mixed-race *mestizos*; blacks whose ancestors were brought from Africa to South America as slaves; and Creoles, white South Americans of mostly Spanish ancestry, some of them claiming proud descent from the original *conquistadores*. Countries such as Peru even have sizable Japanese communities whose forebears arrived as indentured labourers, and who now include Peru's President Alberto Fujimori. Not surprisingly, the mix has produced figures of worldwide renown, including Nobel prize-winners, Chile's two great poets Gabriela Mistral and Pablo Neruda and the Colombian novelist Gabriel García Márquez.

The appeal of the region lies also in the surroundings, for the Andean republics encompass huge contrasts of scenery and climates. In the far south, glaciers slither down the mountainsides of Chile's fjordland, dropping vast icebergs into the ocean. A little farther north, in central Chile, world-class wines are produced on gentler slopes, basking in a temperate, Mediterranean-like warmth. To the north again, on the borders of Chile and Peru, is the Atacama Desert, where in places no rain has fallen within living memory. In landlocked Bolivia, meanwhile, the Andes split into two parallel ranges – the Eastern and Western Cordilleras – with the windswept, treeless plateau of the Altiplano stretched out between them. Its average height is over 12,000 feet above sea level, and at its northern tip, bordering Peru, stretch the chill waters of Lake Titicaca, the highest large lake in the world. The mighty Amazon – the world's second-longest river, after the Nile – rises in the Peruvian Andes and is navigable for 6000-ton, ocean-going vessels as far as the jungle port of Iquitos in eastern Peru. The Andean republics from Bolivia north to Venezuela all contain large hinterlands of still partly untamed Amazonian rain forest. Colombia and Venezuela also include the pampas-like grasslands of the *llanos* – haunts of the fiercely independent *llanero* cowboys – and steaming Caribbean coastlines.

Mineral wealth abounds throughout the region. In the central Andes are the fabled mines of gold and silver that, more than anything else, drew the Spanish to the region. Centuries of ruthless exploitation have exhausted many of them, and South America now produces less than 2 per cent of the world's gold. But places such as Potosí in Bolivia, once famous for its 'mountain of silver' and in the mid-17th century the largest city in the Americas, still have rich veins of other metals – in Potosí's case, tin, copper and lead. Chile boasts Chuquicamata in the Atacama Desert, the largest open-cast copper mine in the world, as well as substantial resources of nitrates, zinc, lead and some oil. Venezuela in the north is one of the world's largest oil-producers, while Colombia has emeralds, nickel, coal and iron ore as well as some oil and natural gas.

Other riches are also there. The cinchona trees of the Amazon jungle produce quinine, for long the chief anti-malarial drug. Rubber made from the sap of the softwood *Hevea brasiliensis* tree created boom times in large parts of the

Amazon region in the late 19th century. Colombia is famous for its coffee (every car entering the country is sprayed against diseases which might attack the coffee crop); Venezuela produces cocoa. The coca plant of the central Andean republics yields a more infamous crop. For centuries, local Indians have chewed its leaves as a stimulant, enabling them to endure hard work on often empty stomachs – but it is also the source of the drug cocaine (a tempting moneyspinner for impoverished peasant farmers). South America was also the original home of the guinea pig (bred for the table in Inca times and before) and its relative the chinchilla, valued for its soft fur. The wool of the llama-like vicuña of the high Andean plateaus is reputed to be the finest in the world.

For the visitor, the region's riches are equally abundant. The old walled city of Cartagena rises from Colombia's Caribbean shore with all the colonial splendour of a port that was once the most important on the Spanish Main. Here, the galleons of Spain's treasure fleets loaded their cargoes of gold and silver for the long, perilous journey back across the Atlantic to Europe. Despite its formidable fortifications, Cartagena was raided several times by English and French freebooters, including Sir Francis Drake in 1586. Cities such as the old Inca capital Cuzco, in Peru, have a wealth of fine Spanish colonial buildings, many of them constructed on Inca foundations. On Cuzco's outskirts, the massive, mortarless stonework of the temple of Sacsahuamán bears witness to the Incas' matchless skills as stonemasons, not to mention the manpower they mobilised during construction – individual stones weigh up to 130 tons. Another of their memorials is the long lost city of Machu Picchu, set in misty solitude on a saddle between jungle-clad mountains – and rediscovered only in 1911.

The centuries have left South America's Andean republics with a heritage of incomparable cultural wealth. In Colombia, for example, the mingling of native Indian, Spanish and African influences has produced traditions of music and dance that have few equals – from the lilting cadences of the *bambuco*, the country's national dance, played on small, 12-stringed *tiple* guitars, to the rhythmic, African-influenced beat of the *currulao*. In the high plateaus of the central Andes, the haunting music of the panpipes is an inevitable accompaniment to the numerous fiestas that punctuate the calendar – themselves testimony to the fertile mixing of cultures.

Life has rarely been easy in the jungles, sparse mountain pastures and dry coastal plains of the Andean region, but the spirit of the peoples who settled there – from the earliest hunter-gatherers arriving over 22,000 years ago, at the end of a gradual migration from Asia across the Bering Strait and down the spine of North and Central America – seems bent towards survival and resilience. The modern world has made its inevitable mark, but an older world long predating the Spanish conquest is never far away: in the villages of the Mapuche Indians of southern Chile, whose ancestors successfully resisted the encroachments of Spanish and then republican forces well into the 19th century; in the troops of pack-bearing llamas driven along mountain tracks, much as they were in Inca times; and in the majestic wheelings at heights of up to 26,000 feet of the Andean condor, the huge black and white vulture that has looked down upon the scene below since long before men ever arrived there.

Peru

The fabled realm of the Incas has lost little of its magic.
Peru may be dogged by political instability and the activities of
Communist guerrillas, but nothing can deprive it of the sheer
splendour of its scenery. The snow-capped peaks of the Andes
rise majestically from narrow coastal plains, and to their east
spread the mysterious jungles of the upper Amazon basin.
Surviving as a memorial to the wonders of Inca civilisation is the
long lost city of Machu Picchu. The people of today, meanwhile,
are moulded by a fertile mix of contrasting traditions.

Previous page: *In the village of Chinchero, the rich colours of the Quechua women's* llicllas *brighten a landscape of whites and ochres. Commerce is the women's domain, as men watch from the church square.*

In his work The Incas, *the French ethnologist A. Métraux wrote about the 'forms of oppression which have made the Incas' descendants the defiant, withdrawn, desperately humble people one meets in the Andes today. Their pride has been broken but not their energy.'*

Of all the Camelidae, *the vicuña has the finest fleece. When subjects paid tribute to their king in Inca times, vicuña cloth was considered the most precious offering. At one time close to extinction, the vicuña now benefits from government protection.*

Universe of the Incas

There are few places on earth more intriguing than the lost world of the Incas, where relics of an empire once almost as large as Europe lie broken and scattered across a landscape of harsh beauty. Modern Peru may be a synonym for bloodshed and poverty; but it is also the key to some of the most enduring mysteries of ancient civilisation.

Though half its territory covers the densely forested Amazon basin, it is the *cordillera* of the Andes, and the extraordinary succession of ancient cultures it has maintained, that fires the imagination. The country stretches 1500 miles along the Pacific coast, and its mountains run from north-west to south-east. Though history and geography have conspired to make Peru one of the most diverse countries in the world, it has just three distinct regions: the coastal lowlands, the Andean *sierra* and the Amazon basin or Montaña.

The Andes rise to 22,000 feet, their jagged peaks and steep canyons surrounding a mineral-rich plateau through which rivers have cut deep, longitudinal valleys. The Amazon forest descends in humid, cloud-wreathed terraces down the eastern flanks of these mountains into a vast tropical plain still prowled by the animals of ancient Inca motifs, the puma and jaguar. West of the mountains, though, lies a coastal desert strip in places more arid than the Sahara, though a clinging winter sea-fog or *garúa* provides moisture to sustain light vegetation.

Such extremes sustain diverse ecosystems and peoples adapted to live in them. Languages and dialects, beliefs and festivals, lifestyles and work ethics, modes of dress and staple foods, change radically from region to region, reflecting the geography of the area and the diverse ethnic origins of the people who live there.

Into the melting pot

Peru is a country of extraordinary ethnic diversity: though more than half its population of 22 million is of pure Indian stock and speaks Quechua, the original Inca language, there are brisk Japanese businessmen, languid Creoles of Hispanic descent, Chinese, blacks, and some 200,000 forest Indians living in the Montaña. Almost half the population lives in the coastal lowlands with another 40 per cent, mostly Quechua-speaking Indians, in the *sierra*. Fifteen per cent of the population speak Aymara, the other Indian language.

Cooperation between the different Indian groups dates back to pre-Columbian times when the great physical divisions of the country had already spawned differences between the regions. The Spaniards introduced another tier of ethnic and cultural variation, and the slaves they imported brought yet another. Together with imported labour from China and, more recently, Japan, all these ethnic strands have been woven into a racial tapestry where mixed heritage is the rule rather than the exception.

Despite the grim reality of life in the *sierra*, the Indians have not lost sight of their long and proud heritage. The two most important pre-Columbian races – the Quechua and the Aymara – live alongside one

Indian myths tell how Manco Capac, the founder of Cuzco, was killed by a white chief who buried his head near Lima. The head, they say, has been growing ever since and one day it will return with a new body, and the Inca empire will be restored.

another in the Puno region in southern Peru and continue the cult of the earth and the elements. Their ancient languages, age-old arts and legends are passed on to succeeding generations. Despite increasing contact with the outside world and modern ways, the indigenous communities of the southern plateau have preserved their animist rites, their rules of generally peaceful coexistence and their celebrations, embracing technical progress only when it does not conflict with their cultural identity. Hence the Roman Catholic church has chosen to graft its rites and feast-days onto the more ancient beliefs.

Unlike many developing countries where traditional dress has become merely a tourist attraction, costume expresses the essence of Peru's Indian societies. The various colours and designs denote membership of a particular group or class, or the possession of certain personal qualities. Differences there are in plenty between the different communities, and yet the Indians living in the region of Lake Titicaca are also united. Indeed, it is this same cultural cohesion that has earned the region its reputation as Peru's most rebellious area: one that boasts an almost messianic belief in the right of the Indians to replace Europeans as the rulers of their own land. What is now above shall one day be below, runs their millennial creed.

These *campesinos* of the highlands practise subsistence agriculture and maintain a distinct culture, though poverty is forcing increasing numbers to migrate to the miseries of the capital, Lima. Yet the Indian fiestas or Catholic holidays are still marked with the full traditional pageantry, dancing, and prodigious drinking. The most spectacular of these festivals, in which hundreds of people dress in Inca costumes, is the Inti Raymi in Cuzco. On such feast days, Inca flutes and an array of costumes depicting jaguars or the stately black

and white Andean vulture, the condor, enliven the seemingly bleak existence, along with magnificent firework displays.

As with most South American Indian families, the woman controls the budget, because she remains on the family plot while her husband travels to find work. It is not that the society is matriarchal – in fact, areas of dominance are more or less evenly divided between

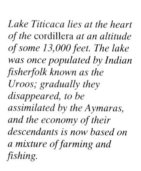

Lake Titicaca is sacred to the Indians of the high plateaus: the first Inca, Manco Capac, set out from one of its islands to found Cuzco; and, perhaps even more impressively, the god Viracocha emerged from its waters to bestow humanity with the gift of civilisation.

Lake Titicaca lies at the heart of the cordillera *at an altitude of some 13,000 feet. The lake was once populated by Indian fisherfolk known as the Uroos; gradually they disappeared, to be assimilated by the Aymaras, and the economy of their descendants is now based on a mixture of farming and fishing.*

men and women – but it is the woman who is seen as the source of stability. It is she who maintains the family's right of tenure, who consolidates the family's place in the community and who ensures the continuity of traditions.

The Andean peasant, who rises at daybreak and walks barefoot – or wearing *ojotas* cut from old tyres – to dig his smallholding, leads an apparently simple,

traditional life. Yet he is the product of many parts. His plough is probably a pre-Hispanic *chaquitajilla*, but the furrows it produces may well be planted with European barley and the field itself most likely belongs to a new agricultural cooperative. A llama bears his burdens, but it is sheep that forage among the stubble after the harvest. There may well be a small Christian cross on top of his house, but all around it there are miniature

Potatoes, here being planted on an island in Lake Titicaca, are the most precious gift the Andean Indians have given to the world. Over the centuries, more than 700 varieties have been developed.

clay models of cattle, bottles and maize – indeed, everything he hopes to receive from the Inca gods to whom he still makes offerings of coca (the shrub whose leaves contain the drug cocaine and have been chewed by the people of the Andes for centuries as a stimulant). He may celebrate his marriage in a Catholic church, but this usually happens long after a civil ceremony, which itself is preceded by the *servinacuy*, a traditional ritual of union.

A glorious history

A procession of women with layered skirts and bowler hats; children in ragged school uniforms; men on horses or mules riding alongside others on bicycles; miners wrapped in traditional ponchos or leatherette jackets with pick-axes over their shoulders: these are the poor but proud inheritors of an empire that blazed briefly across much of South America's western coast. Yet the

Inca empire, abruptly obliterated in 1532, was not the first advanced Andean civilisation.

Modern Peru was first settled about 10,000 years ago and cave paintings in the Tacna area show that Stone Age hunting groups were active around 4000 BC. By 300 BC the so-called Chavín de Huantar culture – named after imposing temple ruins near the village of Chavín de Huantar in central Peru – was active and had developed religious and artistic motifs such as the

stylised jaguar and probably controlled much of northern Peru. Ceramics, metalwork, textiles, archaeological relics and the Nazca Lines of the coastal desert, all provide a catalogue of early Peruvian life up to AD 700, when the Huari empire, the first military force in the Andes, swept through. The Huari were in turn sent into decline around AD 1100 by the rise of the Chimú, who established the first urban societies on the coast, including the adobe city of Chan-Chan whose ruins still spread out over the Moche valley near Trujillo in the north.

Lake Titicaca, now situated largely in Bolivia, was the literal birthplace of the Inca empire. Legend says the first Incas – Manco Capac and his sister-wife Mama Ocllo – appeared on one of the lake's islands. The Incas

The Indian women of the sierra lead a hard life. Not only do they do all the domestic work; they also have sole responsibility for the children, since their menfolk frequently have to leave home to find work.

Andean women spin wool as they tend their flocks.

called their empire Tahuantinsayo, or the 'four parts' in Quechua. According to accounts given to the Spanish, the empire achieved about two-thirds of its final size under Inca Pachacuti, who came to power in 1438.

By the end of the 15th century, Pachacuti's successor, Topa Inca Yupanqui (1471-1493), had built an empire that stretched from Ecuador in the north to Chile in the south. He even established a second capital in Quito. Civil war broke that empire apart, however, when Yupanqui's successor Huayna Capac tried to split what was by then the largest native empire of the Americas, controlling an estimated 12 million people. Much of the expansion was simply by military conquest: battles were frequently brutal invasions of neighbouring territories, crushing any resistance.

The war between Huayna Capac's two sons, Huáscar

In the southern Andes, regional costume is still worn. Contrary to popular belief, this dress has nothing to do with Inca tradition, but is an imitation of the Spanish fashions of centuries ago.

whelmed by the top-heavy bureaucracy that was running their diffuse empire and Old World epidemics such as smallpox and influenza had preceded the *conquistadores*.

The Incas' enduring achievement is their public architecture, fine stonemasonry and superb engineering. How was this achieved without benefit of the wheel? Perfect joints in their massive masonry, towns laid out with broad avenues and smaller streets and seemingly impregnable fortresses such as Sacsayhuamán, were all

and Atahualpa, debilitated an already over-extended empire. However, it was an extraordinary meeting on November 15, 1532 that was to change the continent's destiny. The victorious Atahualpa was marching his army south to claim his throne at Cuzco when in Cajamarca he collided with no more than 180 dirty, famished Spanish desperadoes, with 30 horses and a few cannon, under the command of an illegitimate former swineherd, Francisco Pizarro.

That such a complex and highly developed society could have been so swiftly undone by a handful men on horseback is still an enigma in mankind's study of the fall of empires. But the Incas were already over-

Wherever practical, traditional Indian crops of the sierra *have been replaced by plantations of European origin. Here, small irrigated plots are devoted to cereal-growing.*

put together in the most difficult terrain, as in the Andean citadel of Machu Picchu.

Pizarro's first act on meeting the surprised Inca army was to seize Atahualpa. When a huge ransom in gold and silver was handed over, the Spaniard promptly had the Inca emperor strangled and he then marched to the capital Cuzco, which surrendered without a fight. Pizarro's overthrow of the Inca is usually attributed to luck rather than cunning. In fact, he was working to a plan hatched as far back as 1510 when he sailed with

Hernán Cortés. During his third expedition, in 1526, he began exploring southwards from Panama and first touched upon the riches of the Inca empire's northern outposts. Equipped with fresh soldiers, new equipment and a royal mandate to conquer, he set off again in 1530 for northern Peru, where he founded a town on the coast before marching straight inland to his fateful encounter at Cajamarca.

The decline of the Inca state was swift. Manco Inca, who had been installed as a puppet by the Spanish,

rebelled in 1536, setting up a jungle retreat at Vitcos, but he was killed and resistance crumbled. Nor was Pizarro to enjoy the spoils of conquest: he was assassinated in 1541 and a year later his brother, Gonzalo, overthrew the first Spanish viceroy sent to Lima to establish order among warring *conquistadores*.

Cradle of civilisations

Any journey to the origins of Peru must begin at Lake Titicaca, the cradle of the Andes' two great civilisations – Tiahuanaco and the Inca.

This is the most densely populated rural area in Peru. Situated some 13,000 feet above sea level, the lake tempers the otherwise harsh conditions. Periodically it floods and irrigates the fields; it provides fish which is a staple of the local diet; and it supports *totora*, the reed which is the main building material for the Puno Indians. They use it to make boats, to construct small islands on the lake, and to build houses on those islands. Their floating islands, some as large as a football pitch, are still found on the northern end of the lake. Dense layers of the *totora* reed separate these people and their damp homes from the icy blue waters of the lake; they also make canoes of bundled reeds similar to that that

the Norwegian explorer Thor Heyerdahl built to make his epic Ra voyage across the Atlantic from Morocco in 1969.

Taquile Island, reached by boat from Puno and lying close to the centre of the lake, has remained unchanged due to the absence of roads or electricity. This island's Quechua-speaking population embrace traditional clothing and customs. The peaceful Inca terraces and the ruins of an ancient temple are enlivened by rowdy festivals in August.

Life on the lakeshore is hard. Some Indians have been attracted to the lake by the acute land shortage in the surrounding regions, others by the lake's tourist

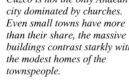

Cuzco is not the only Andean city dominated by churches. Even small towns have more than their share, the massive buildings contrast starkly with the modest homes of the townspeople.

Andean civilisations are characterised by their skill in managing water and devising ingenious irrigation systems.

potential. But the struggle for survival is intense, and no natural resource is wasted. Most families have a few cattle, penned on the shore by *totora* fences. These unfortunate animals, with nothing but reeds for grazing, are sold as soon as they have put on a few pounds to buy food to supplement the crops grown on small family plots.

The struggle for land in Puno is intense. On the Cachi-Pucara peninsula, where thousands of tiny brick-and-mud houses, with roofs of thatch or corrugated iron, are crammed together on the shore of the lake, it is impossible for these Indians to be self-sufficient through agriculture. They have diversified into crafts such as weaving, basket-making, ceramics, making carnival masks and costumes – indeed, anything to provide a few extra *intis* for the family coffers. Puno itself dates from 1668 and is the largest Peruvian town on the lakeshore. Seedy and windswept, the main attractions of Puno are the handicrafts and the November festival, when the Indians celebrate the coming of Manco Capac, the first Inca, with a water-borne procession.

Despite their best efforts, the Puno Indians suffer from grinding poverty and are therefore prone to all kinds of trafficking. Puno is the smuggling capital of Peru: a profession undertaken mainly by the women of the region. They conceal all sorts of goods, under their petticoats, in the folds of their blouses or in their *llicllas* (cloth wraps tied around their necks for carrying children or produce).

Juliaca, on the road to both Cuzco and Arequipa, is a typical *sierra* town, whose absence of colour or architectural charm is more than made up for by the astonishing spectacle of a Sunday market when the Aymara and Quechua Indians crowd into the square. This is Peru's largest outdoor market, and at 12,100 feet its highest town of any size.

The carefully restored convent of Santa Catalina in Arequipa was opened to the public in 1970, after 390 years of isolation. With an area of 8 square miles, the convent is, in effect, a self-contained small town.

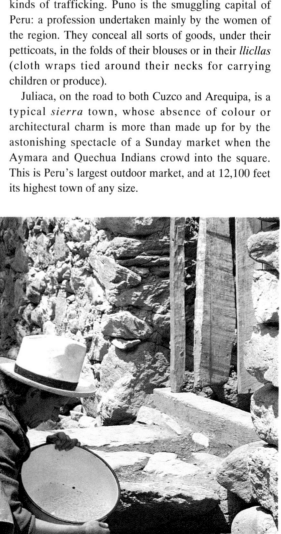

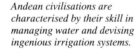

Beyond the blues, greens and ochres of Lake Titicaca stretches an immense, bleak plateau. This is the *puna*, a desert zone of tough, yellow grass which leads to the Andes. Because of the altitude, some 16,000 feet above sea level, people have to fight for breath up here; as a result, the undulating tablelands are only sparsely populated by shepherds who live in scattered communities of conical or rectangular huts, or in agricultural cooperatives.

Aristocratic Arequipa

Farther east, towards Arequipa and the Pacific, the ethnic and cultural mix becomes more complex. The valleys beyond the Andes' western watershed reflect a rich combination of Indian and Spanish tradition. These valleys are particularly charming, because of the area's spectacular scenery and because the isolation of each

American Indians were responsible for introducing Europeans to maize. The crop is thought to have originated in southern Mexico, where it was bred from robust, self-germinating grass. From Mexico, it was exported to other parts of pre-Columbian America.

The calabash is perhaps the most ancient plant cultivated in the Americas. Long before the introduction of pottery, its fruit was used to make all manner of strange vessels.

valley has allowed it to evolve its own style. For example, the valley of Río Colca (95 miles north of Arequipa) opens into the world's deepest canyon. Gorges plunge down 13,000 feet, flanked on either side by snow-capped volcanoes, and condors sweep down from the ridges. The small valley is pitted with some 60 craters – some no bigger than a house, others the size of a tower block.

The Peruvian coast is, for the most part, desert: a narrow, arid band between the Andes and the Pacific. Around Arequipa, however, stretches an immense, gently sloping plateau. Arequipa itself sits some 7700 feet above sea-level, on the edge of a desert of volcanic sand, lava and ash. The area is crossed by several small rivers supporting a strange paradise in the midst of such a wilderness. The climate is sublime and, where cultivation is practical, the land fertile. Spanish colonists happened upon this region and soon established Arequipa as one of Peru's principal cities; it quickly became the market garden for the whole south and south-west of the country.

Set against the backdrop of the volcano El Misti, Arequipa has developed a taste for intellectual life and the arts. Even its physical appearance is distinctive. The entire city is built from *sillar*, a soft white volcanic stone which is found in abundance in the area and has earned Arequipa the nickname 'the white city'.

Despite the destruction wrought by recent earthquakes and despite new residential quarters which crowd in on the old town, Arequipa retains its colonial charm. The city is effectively controlled by a handful of old patrician families, descendants of the first Hispanic settlers. It is extremely difficult to make any real contact with them because, beneath a veneer of courtesy and benevolence, a deeply entrenched class-consciousness keeps them aloof. Yet their influence is everywhere: in the city's architecture, and in its customs, values and aspirations. The extraordinary Santa Catalina walled convent, for example, is a veritable Andalusian citadel. Built in 1580, soon after the Conquest, the convent isolated its 450 nuns from the world in a miniature city complete with tiny streets and courtyards. A few nuns still live in the convent, which was beautifully restored in 1970 and is now open to the public. Arequipa's churches are a delight: the cathedral on the Plaza de Armas was rebuilt in the 19th century but La Campañía has a striking and original façade. La Recoleta, a 17th-century Franciscan monastery, also suffered damage and has been rebuilt. But the influence of the ancient Indian civilisations is here too. For all their artwork glorifying the opulence of the Spanish republic, the churches and seignorial houses also incorporate decorative designs, symbols and artefacts of the ancient Andean cultures.

Seen from the Pan-American Highway that swings northwards from Arequipa along the coast, the desert is an astonishing, if inhospitable, place. The greatest enigma is to be found at Nazca, where strange markings in the earth and rock were first detected from the air in the 1920s. Just how could a culture that vanished around AD 600 have exercised the geometric control necessary to draw a condor with a 300-foot wing-span?

The Nazca valley and Pampa de San José are almost rainless: over the millennia the sun oxidised stones on

In the temperate regions of America, maize is the staple food. The grain can be eaten whole or ground into a flour; it is also used to make an alcoholic drink called chicha.

The clothes worn by this Indian woman from Cuzco are woven on a loom like the one she is using. Many of the decorative designs of today date back to the Incas.

the surface, making them appear darker than those below. The Nazcas, who followed the Paracas culture from around AD 200, simply removed lines of these darker stones to make their extraordinary drawings. A monkey with a curly tail, a condor, a lizard and a whale – none of these figures is less than 150 feet across. The lines and geometric shapes were probably drawn later, around the 8th century. Many of the motifs in these ground drawings also adorn ceramics, textiles, and gold worked by the Nazcas. Colourful theories of alien intelligence have been brushed aside by modern archaeologists who believe the lines represent a complex astronomical calendar. Flights are readily available and visitors may draw their own conclusions. Other Nazca

relics can be seen at the Chauchilla cemetery some 18 miles away, where bleached bones and ceramic funerary urns lie in the desert. At Carhuachi, the old Nazca capital, there are more funerary relics.

The Spanish and the other whites of the *haciendas* created their own Creole culture. They planted vines and, while Peruvian wine has never rivalled that of Chile, they did manage to produce an exceptional brandy, called *pisco*. This drink is the preserve of the Peruvian elite and its production is a mainstay of the economy of Ica and the south coast.

Situated on the Pan-American Highway, Ica is the centre of Peru's wine industry; it holds a wine festival every March, and opens a number of *bodegas* or wineries

The shape of these vessels, displayed at Tyobamba market, is Hispanic. The introduction of the potter's wheel to the region did little to improve the quality of Indian pottery, but rather encouraged the supplanting of their beautiful ancient designs.

to the public. Ica was also a centre for Nazca and Paracas culture; as a result, the town's archaeological museum contains many fine examples of textiles and ceramics.

Creole culture – the gracious if languid existence of the predominantly white descendants of Spanish colonial masters – would not have evolved at all without the magnificent houses of the old *haciendas*, whose wide patios, arches and spacious rooms were designed for large social gatherings. But the days of this ostentatious lifestyle appear to be numbered. Agrarian reforms, which were introduced into the region in the 1970s, forced the rural elite into decline and, in some regions, it has disappeared altogether.

Pisco, which gave its name to Peru's national drink (a kind of brandy), was once a whaling port. Today it is better known for its proximity to the Paracas peninsula and for the archaeological site at Cerro Colorado, which was uncovered by the Peruvian archaeologist Julio C. Tello. His find in 1925 was among the most important in the history of Andean archaeology. The high point of Paracas culture was its weaving. Embroidered with hundreds of tiny figures, cotton and wool were woven into richly coloured textiles and mantles of extraordinary intricacy, probably to accompany burials. The main burial sites suggest that the Paracas culture was divided into two main phases: the early Cavernas (300 BC-AD 200) and then the later Necropolis phase, which ended around AD 800. Tello's excavation of Necropolis tombs produced around 400 textile bundles, many of which are in Lima, but some can be seen at the local museum. Today the peninsula and the nearby Ballestas islands, which were once a source of guano (bird-dung fertiliser), are wildlife reserves where sea-lions, penguins and other sea birds may be observed.

All the traditional Indian staples can still be found in the market at Cuzco: maize, potatoes, beans and llama meat. But there are new things too, such as rice, garlic, onions, beef and dairy products.

A coca seller in Pisac market. Indians chew the leaves to stave off hunger, thirst and exhaustion. The effect of the leaves is much milder than that of refined cocaine from which the drug barons make their fortunes.

Once a year, on the feast day of a village's patron saint, the daily routine gives way to celebration. Everyone dons their best clothes and joins in the dancing and drunken revelry.

October 7 is the feast day in Calca, near Cuzco. The celebrations incorporate a mixture of Catholic and pre-Columbian mythology, as the figures of God and Christ are identified with the ancient Inca sun god.

Roads to Cuzco

You can still take the traditional mountain roads from the Pacific to the Andes – the same trade routes that linked the coast to the mountains and the jungle beyond. Indeed, they are still used for commercial purposes because the Pan-American Highway, along the Peruvian coast, was completed too recently to have seriously disrupted traditional patterns.

In pre-Columbian times, relays of foot messengers, or *chasquis*, passed daily along the steep footpaths between Chala and Cuzco, bringing fresh fish for the Inca tables. The Incas also constructed an extraordinary network of roads along the entire length of the crest of the Andes. But the Spanish, with their drive for exports, reverted to the old roads that linked the mountain cities to the ports.

Water is an obsession in Peru. Even in the Andes, with its ample rainfall, people have always had difficulty in maintaining an adequate supply. It is a subject that is deeply entrenched in Indian mythology and custom. The Indians still perform their 'water rites'; for example, the annual 'festival of water' in Puquio, when the irrigation channels are cleared, is an occasion for peasants to reaffirm their links with the past and with the pre-Columbian *ayllus* – a social group based on kinship and joint land ownership.

Shortage of water also explains the demise of Ayacucho. Now a small provincial town in the heart of Peru's most arid and inhospitable region, it was once the centre of the Huari culture that predated the Incas. The capital of an Andean empire that flourished until around AD 900, ancient Ayacucho was a centre of artistic innovation and qualifies as one of the very first true pre-Columbian cities. Many of the old colonial houses in modern Ayacucho have also survived, with their porticos, balconies and patios. These splendid buildings give the town an Hispanic grandeur which sits uneasily amidst the squalor of the region.

More recently, Ayacucho has acquired a different kind of fame – for the politically radical students at its university and the harsh measures taken by the local authorities to keep them in check. Peru's Communist *Senero Luminoso* (Shining Path) guerrillas have been active in the area, and the military have responded with strictly enforced curfews.

Navel of the world

According to Inca legend, when the gods created the valleys around Cuzco (or Qosqo as it is now officially known), they designated the area the navel of the world. Even today, the Cuzco region is clearly influenced by the distinctive values and aspirations of the pre-Columbian era. For example, in every village people are strictly divided into opposite groups: high and low, *hanan* and *hurin*, male and female. This system of division governs almost everything – the organisation of

In Ayaviri, between Cuzco and Puno, the festival of llamas and the festival of shepherds are celebrated jointly. Shepherds wear woollen masks to protect their faces from the icy winds.

Pre-Columbian cultures had a whole range of wind instruments, to which were added the Hispanic stringed instruments, such as the guitar, harp and charango. All of these were incorporated into Andean music.

The Christian conversion of the Indians gave birth to a whole new style of religious art. The imported baroque style was adapted into a proliferation of new forms, lavishly decorated with gilt.

The cemeteries of the Andean Indians resemble small houses surmounted with crosses. In modern towns, only the rich can afford a mausoleum or vault; the coffins of poorer people are slotted, one above the other, into recesses in vast walls.

work, the allocation of land, the choice of spouse, and even dress codes.

Beneath a veneer of Catholic devotion, the Indians of Cuzco still cherish the tutelary gods of their ancestors. The route of the *Qoillur Riti*, a popular pilgrimage, is lined with Christian places of worship, images of the Virgin and crucifixes. But in reality it is Ausangate, a towering snow-capped peak, that receives the tributes of the Indians. It is no coincidence that, in Cuzco, Corpus Christi, the most important date in the Catholic calendar, happens to fall on the same date – June 14 – that the Incas used to parade the mummified remains of their ancestors through the streets of the city.

If Christian beliefs have been superimposed on Incan myths, then everywhere in Cuzco colonial buildings quite literally rest on more ancient foundations. And below those Inca stones are the relics of the Huari and even earlier cultures.

Pachacutec, the Inca king who in the mid-1400s began a wave of territorial expansion, was the true father of the city his people knew as 'the navel of the world'. It was he who laid out the central plaza and built the Coricancha Palace and its Golden Courtyard close to the central Plaza de Armas. When Francisco Pizarro entered the city on November 8, 1533, the palace had already been stripped of tons of treasure by his advance guard. Once the Spanish had looted its riches and begun to pull down some of the Inca buildings to make way for churches, they lost interest in Cuzco, and Pizarro transferred his capital to Lima in 1536. Since then Cuzco has mellowed into one of the continent's most fascinating and delightful cities, most of which can be explored on foot.

Steep cobbled streets that squeeze past the massive stones of former temples or palaces, make up part of a complex city plan that originally represented the puma, a sacred animal. The largest of the colonial buildings in the central Plaza de Armas is the cathedral, which dates from 1559 and whose interior is decorated with paintings from the famous 17th-century Cuzco School of art. The Triunfo Chapel commemorates the Spanish victory over an Inca counterattack in 1536.

The Cuzco artists owed much to Bishop Mollinedo, who arrived in Peru in 1672 with a large collection which included two works by the Greek-born painter El Greco. Mollinedo was responsible for much of Cuzco's colonial rebuilding and did much to encourage local artists and craftsmen. One of the most impressive of their works is an enormous canvas, now hanging in the Triunfo Chapel, which depicts in dramatic and gory detail the great earthquake which struck Cuzco in 1650.

The Coricancha Palace, with its extraordinarily precise stonework still in place, once contained temples dedicated to the moon and to the stars. Hatun Rumioc, the 12-sided stone after which a street is named, is close to Inca Roca's palace, which today houses the magnificent Religious Art Museum.

Cuzco's inhabitants live in accordance with the rhythms of the seasons. The Plaza de Armas can suddenly fill with thousands of peasants and students protesting at price rises or inadequate public services. Endless processions take place there, too: to venerate the image of the 'God of earthquakes' and to seek protection from possible further destruction. Here also you can still see signs announcing: 'Maids wanted in Lima', or 'We are hiring *peones* for the coffee harvest at La Convención'.

Close to Cuzco is the Urubamba Valley, also known as the Sacred Valley. The most impressive, and the closest, Inca site is the old fort at Sacsayhuamán, another work by the Inca Pachacuti. According to the 16th-century Spanish chronicler Cieza de León, around 20,000 workers helped to build it. Some 4000 of them were kept busy quarrying the stone; another 6000 used rollers to haul the stones up to the site. About 10,000 men were employed on site fitting the stones together. Following the city layout of a puma, the fort once represented the head, with its zigzag walls forming the animal's teeth. Though its walls still seem massive, only a small portion remain today because the Spaniards used so much of the stone for their own building – leaving behind 300-ton blocks they found too heavy to move. These huge stones are fitted with such precision that a knife blade cannot be inserted between them.

In the month of June, during the winter solstice celebrations, the festival of *Inti Raymi* is held in the

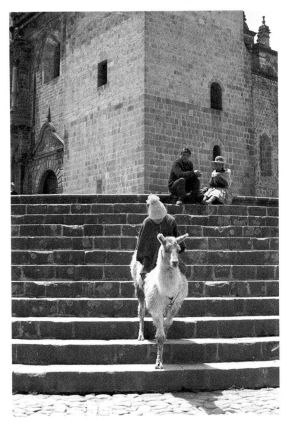

It is rare for a llama to carry a rider, since they cannot bear heavy loads. But like their cousins, the camels, they do have great stamina and endurance.

grass-covered plaza. Carved seats on the hillside opposite offered the Incas a grandstand view of complex rituals for which priests and performers would have been adorned with brilliant plumage taken from birds in the foothills of the Amazon forest.

The old Inca terraces in the Sacred Valley above Pisac are still under cultivation. The Pisac ruins, reached by a winding track from the town, are an exciting preparation for the glories of Machu Picchu. The ruins, perched above the town, include temples of the Sun and Moon, and a necropolis carved into the hillside. At the very centre of the Temple of the Sun is an extraordinary sundial, the *Intihuatana*, from which the Inca priests were able to make precise astronomical calculations. The Spanish went out of their way to try to destroy all these stones because of their significance to Inca culture.

Ollantaytambo, about 35 miles from Pisac, is an important Inca site with a massive temple-fortress. The modern town – built on the Inca foundations – is the only one that retains its pre-Columbian layout. This was the site of one of the Incas' few military triumphs against the Spanish, in 1537, during the abortive rebellion of the Spanish puppet Inca Manco. On this occasion, Manco's forces – who included archers from local jungle peoples – outnumbered the Spanish forces so massively that the Spanish decided on discretion rather than valour, and withdrew hastily, leaving much of their equipment behind them.

The Incas' lost city

The valley is the starting point for the famous Inca Trail to Machu Picchu – a three-day hike through a national park that allows visitors to see some Inca ruins, cloud-forest and spectacular landscapes not visible to those who take the train to Machu Picchu. A steady stream of hikers, equipped with tents, cooking materials and food, wind up the muddy paths, scale the Inca stairways and gasp at the spectacular view over a 13,700-foot pass. On the way the trail passes a string of ruins and small villages. At Puyopatamarca, chilly water still cascades through six ceremonial Inca baths: at Sayacjmarca vegetation overwhelms the ancient stonework. Intipunku, the Gateway of the Sun, is the final stop on the trail before Machu Picchu. It is within sight of Machu Picchu and its nearby thermal springs for foot-weary hikers.

In 1911, the American Hiram Bingham located the abandoned, vegetation-enshrouded city 7875 feet above sea level on the eastern slopes of the Andes, overlooking the Urubamba Valley. Machu Picchu, the 'Lost City of the Incas', may be Peru's greatest treasure but its precise history is still unknown. This was probably not the city to which the Spanish finally tracked the last Inca kings in 1572, but its soaring grandeur and mystery make Machu Picchu one of the world's most important archaeological sites. The location on the eastern borders of the Inca empire may mean that the city (named after a nearby peak) was a fort; but it clearly had significant religious and ceremonial functions as well.

The most famous relic in this city which, together with its agricultural terracing, appears to be carved out of the mountainsides, is the *Intihuatana,* a sundial enclosed by curved walls and trapezoidal windows. When Bingham first arrived, this must have been a ghostly place; then there were still Inca mummies in the Temple of the Sun and all but a few local peasants had forgotten its existence. Even today the hubbub that follows the arrival of the daily tourist train from Cuzco, cannot entirely shatter the majesty of Machu Picchu.

Equally magical is the climb up the nearby peak of Huayna Picchu ('Young Height'), which gives superb views over Machu Picchu and the surrounding jungle with further, snow-capped peaks rising beyond. A trail from the peak leads to a grotto, overlooking the Urubamba river, which houses an Inca Temple of the Moon.

Wherever it is impossible to use animals for ploughing, Andean peasants use the ancient chaquitajilla. *This consists of a heavy prodding stick equipped with a metal blade and two crossbars. One is for the planter's left hand; the other is pushed with the foot.*

These foundations on the mountainside overlooking Cuzco are all that remains of the fortress of Sacsayhuamán, which was torn down by the conquistadores. *It was once a superb example of Inca building skills, constructed of huge stone blocks cut into polyhedrals; yet each of these complex blocks fitted one another precisely without the use of mortar.*

Forest Living and the Cultures of the North

The mountains of Peru once sheltered the Inca civilisation but the most famous inhabitants of Peru's lowlands, who gave their name to one of the world's mightiest rivers, never existed at all. The Amazons were a fearsome tribe of female warriors which flourished only in the jungle-warped imaginations of a small group of Spanish *conquistadores*.

In 1541 Francisco de Orellana, the commander of the first expedition to descend the Amazon, guaranteed himself lasting fame by taking with him a chronicler, Friar Gaspar de Carvajal. As his boat drifted towards the Amazon river's mouth on the Atlantic, the friar's imagination was busy with images that owed more to his classical education than to reality. 'These women are very white and tall, and have hair very long and braided and wound about the head, and they are very robust and go about naked . . . doing as much fighting as ten Indian men,' he wrote. When it came to long hair, he and his fellows may have confused long-haired (but male) Indian warriors with women.

This first recorded journey through the Montaña – the forested Amazon plain below the Andean foothills that makes up half of modern Peru – was followed by fruitless attempts to find these sirens, before Spanish attention moved from lowland myth to upland gold; the Amazon was for a time left in peace.

Europeans did not fully penetrate the low-lying areas of the Peruvian Amazon until the late 19th century. Neither the Incas nor their Spanish conquerors ever established settlements in the region, despite the best attempts of the military, missionaries and traders. During the Victorian age, however, the great demand for rubber encouraged adventurers to probe the Indian territories, rich in *Hevea brasiliensis* rubber trees. The rubber barons were soon followed by cattlemen, lumberjacks, gold prospectors and collectors of wild animals and rare plants. These successive waves had one thing in common – their driving force was instant enrichment regardless of environmental or social cost.

These cycles of seemingly miraculous discovery, followed by exploitation, indifference and then indigence, are characteristic of Peru's turbulent history.

Iquitos is built on high ground and is one of the few places in the lower Amazon not to flood. In the crowded suburbs, however, houses are built on stilts, and canoes are the only mode of transport during the wet season.

It achieved independence from Spain in 1824, under the leadership of the Argentine-born 'Liberator' José de San Martín (and with a little help from the freebooting British naval officer Lord Cochrane). But the first civilian government only came to power in 1872. Spain, its former colonial master, once tried to invade it, while Peruvian help for Bolivia in the 1879-83 war against Chile led to the loss of parts of the mineral-rich Atacama Desert. During this century Peru has also had disputes with neighbouring Ecuador over the ownership of the Montaña. Peru's few attempts at democracy have been swamped by its succession of coups and dictatorships.

In the early 1960s, the military handed over power to the leftist *Alianza Popular Revolucionaria Americana* (APRA) but then seized it back in 1968, overthrowing President Fernando Belaúnde Terry. He was returned to power in 1980 and in 1985 handed over to his successor

In a Shipibo village of the Amazon, this Indian is weaving on a small loom tied around her waist. Beside her is a ball of cotton thread from her spindle.

Alán García Pérez, despite a background of economic chaos and mounting terrorist insurgence. García's administration was blackballed internationally for his refusal to pay debts and, by the 1990 elections, the country was sliding into economic and social chaos. For example, per capita income in 1985 was the same as it was in 1965, while by 1989 inflation had reached 8000 per cent and more than half the workforce was jobless. Peru's conservative elite thought they had found a saviour in Mario Vargas Llosa, the country's best-known novelist, but as presidential candidate he was no match for Alberto Fujimori, a little-known university professor of Japanese descent who was elected as Peru's new leader.

With the army's backing, Fujimori set out to deal with Peru's greatest threat, the ruthless *Sendero Luminoso* (Shining Path) guerrilla movement, which had first emerged in the early 1980s. Despite the imprisonment in 1992 of its leader Abimael Guzmán, the movement continues to render some parts of the country unsafe, particularly for travellers, who are regarded as legitimate targets. It mixes the ideological extremism of China's Cultural Revolution with the cruelty of pre-Columbian societies. Its ideologues – white left-wing intellectuals – have grafted the Maoist rhetoric of class struggle onto Indian millennial beliefs about the overthrow of post-colonial society and a return to pre-Columbian values. During a bloody struggle between *Sendero,* the armed forces and the *ronderos* (peasant militia), there has been great brutality on both sides, and more than 20,000 people have been killed. Today, *Sendero* guerrillas are believed to have close links with the drug cartels.

A mosaic of roofs

Always enthralling, and often forbidding, the Amazon is a strange world. The native population was almost wiped out long ago by the confiscation of their lands, enslavement to the rubber exporters, imported diseases, and by the corruption of their culture. Some live a semi-nomadic existence deep in the jungle; others struggle to keep their own land, working as *peones*, servants,

The Indians of the Amazon traditionally roof their houses with the leaves of the shapaja palm. In recent years, however, corrugated iron has been widely used.

craftsmen or, most degrading of all, as token Indians for the benefit of tourists.

To descend from the Andean capital of Cuzco into the Amazon region is to travel to a different world, with new landscapes, cultures, languages, family structures, customs and costumes. Perhaps nothing is so indicative of the difference in values between the cultures of the mountain and the plain as their architecture. The Incas were superb stonemasons, constructing their buildings from massive, precision-cut blocks which they then assembled without mortar. And though modern Andean society lacks the skill or cheap labour to emulate these skills, the old blocks are nevertheless recycled to produce distinctive stone constructions.

In the coastal region, meanwhile, the main building material is mud, and the ancient technique of *pisé* – firmly packed earth – is used to raise thick walls. Adobe bricks – made of mud and straw – are also widely used; they are combined with walls of split bamboo fastened onto a wooden framework and plastered with mud. The Moche pyramids and the Chan Chan archaeological remains near Trujillo bear witness to the antiquity of the *pisé* and adobe construction methods. Even today, people continue to build and restore houses in the same fashion.

The people of the Amazon, in contrast, have no stone and no taste for mud dwellings. The rich jungle vegetation provides all their raw materials. Buildings are constructed from wooden planks in the towns and larger villages; stakes, tree trunks and bark in the hamlets; and wooden piles just about everywhere.

Inside her house, built on stilts, this Indian sits on a floor made of pona palm and prepares maize. Along with cassava, groundnuts and sweet potatoes, this cereal is a staple for Amazon Indians.

The fine geometrical designs favoured by the Shipibo Indians are of ancient origin. They have been linked to the designs of the great Marajó civilisation which flourished around AD 500 at the mouth of the Amazon in what is now Brazil.

Shipibo women give birth hanging from a tree branch. Some Shipibo communities still continue the ancient practice of deforming their babies' skulls by pressing them against padded boards.

Traditional Amazonian roofs of palm leaf are more appropriate to the climate of the region than any modern material. The shapes of Amazon palm roofs vary greatly according to the geometry of the building, which in turn is determined by the number of families living in it. Some are circular, others rectangular or square, but in all cases the roof slopes steeply to allow a run-off for the heavy rainfall.

This big cat is known throughout the world by its Quechua name – the puma. Sometimes called the American lion, it is much smaller than its African cousin.

Forest cultures

Peruvians know the Amazon as the *selva* (jungle): the jungle which stretches up into the Andes is called the *selva alta* (high jungle) or the *ceja de selva* (the jungle's eyebrow). In places its twisted, lichen-covered limbs poke through the mists at heights of more than 10,000 feet, but the main surge of vegetation starts several thousand feet lower. In the brighter light, and on more even ground, the vegetation grows straight and the forest floor is a mass of ferns and orchids.

The eastern slopes of the Andes have traditionally been a battleground and a melting pot of the Andean and Amazonian peoples, each of whom has won and then lost control of this much-coveted region.

Today, the fringes of the eastern *selva alta* are divided into large plantations of coffee, cocoa, tea, fruit and coca. Higher up, peasants clear smaller plots on the steep slopes and cultivate them for a few seasons until the soil, no longer protected by the trees, becomes too severely eroded to sustain crops.

It is here, too, that the long chain from coca leaf to refined cocaine begins. Despite domestic and international efforts to stem the flow, coca has become Peru's most valuable export in both its raw and refined state. The profit coca brings to the local peasants is so great that no other crop can rival it – even when subsidised. Today, the narcotics trade is rotting the very fabric of society in the *selva alta;* now the only respected authority is that of the drug barons.

The lifestyle of the local people depends entirely on whether or not they are involved in the drug rings – comfort co-exists with abject poverty. The whisky and saddles of lamb favoured by the traffickers contrast sharply with the cassava and rice of the coffee growers.

Sometimes the lifestyles produce incongruous sights, such as a peasant in poncho and *ojotas* sitting at the wheel of a new Cadillac.

Scattered along the banks of the rivers, *mestizo* (mixed-race) peasants survive by cultivating temporary plots of burned land and patches of alluvial soil, which are regularly enriched by floods. Their life, diet and work closely resembles that of the full-blooded Indians: houses are built on stilts and are open to the elements. They live a semi-nomadic existence, torn between the constant search for better land and the need to be near schools where their children can receive some sort of education – the only passport out of this world of grinding poverty.

Both the Indians and the river-dwellers live by exploiting the jungle – furs, timber and rare animals – and have become an integral part of a mercantile system which is rapidly destroying their homes. They take their bounty to river traders, nicknamed *retagones* (hagglers), who travel the waterways in motorised canoes, loaded with salt, sugar, cloth, trinkets and alcohol for barter.

The Amazon has few real towns, and those that exist are little more than trading posts, with muddy roads,

The sloth owes its name to the fact that it spends a great deal of its time in a state of near-immobility, hanging from a branch and munching leaves. Its immobility is, in fact, a self-defence mechanism.

Left: *In the wet season, when the lowlands of the Amazon are swamped by floodwater, the inhabitants travel and hunt in canoes.*

A young Yagua Indian gets ready for the kill. His prey is most likely a monkey hiding among the banana leaves.

As well as the bow and arrow, Amazon Indians use blowpipes with poison darts. In the background is a maloca, *a large communal dwelling.*

houses of planks – or more recently cement and corrugated iron – and a general store. The infrastructure is usually poor or non-existent, and fresh water is typically brought in by hawkers and hauled by donkeys.

Rubber wealth

The tropical forest is scattered with rubber trees and tropical timber trees such as ebony and mahogany. Rubber was the reason for the founding of Puerto Maldonado, the southern capital of the largely uninhabited province of Madre de Dios. Like other Amazon towns, it has survived booms in rubber, timber, oil and gold – though of course the surrounding forest has not.

Seemingly tireless under their loads, the Indians of the sierra *follow one of the paths which criss-cross the flanks of the mountains. This network of tracks is the only means of communication between isolated mountain villages.*

A vast range of colourful flowers flourish in the clear air of the Andes. Here, bougainvilleas provide a dazzling crown for a whitewashed wall.

Puerto Maldonado was the location for *Fitzcarraldo*, filmed by Werner Herzog. This half-fictional Irish freebooter dreamed of recreating the late Victorian elegance of the Brazilian rubber city Manaus in one of the world's more inaccessible spots. Because the rapids in the Madeira river made access to the Amazon down the Madre de Dios river impossible, Fitzcarraldo's rubber – and his boat – had to be hauled overland to the Ucayali river and thence to Iquitos.

Peru is now taking the issue of conservation seriously, and parks protect the astonishing diversity of flora and fauna of the Madre de Dios region, one of the least developed areas in the Amazon basin. The Tambopata-Candamo reserve and the larger Manu National Park provide scientists with opportunities to study the Andean cloud forest and the rain forest itself. Visitors are offered treks organised from Cuzco, or travel by canoe to stay in forest lodges beside the river.

Pucallpa, on the banks of the Ucayali, is bigger than most Amazon towns, but it is little more developed due to increased *Sendero* guerrilla activity along the main road to Lima. Pucallpa has also waited in vain for the planned extension of Brazil's BR-364 highway, which would connect it directly to the Atlantic ports and industries. Instead, it can be reached only by boat from Iquitos, or by air. Situated at the foot of the Andes, it resembles a giant shanty town in the process of development. Industry consists mainly of the mass-production of chipboard. The lake of Yarinacocha, a short canoe ride from Pucallpa, is a centre for wildlife and Indian handicrafts.

Sources of the Amazon

At its 150-mile-wide mouth, the Amazon's tide rises more than 18 feet, and its muddy discharge discolours the Atlantic Ocean for hundreds of miles. Yet its sources in the Peruvian Andes near the Pacific Ocean are very different: the river's headstreams form little more than 100 miles from the west coast.

Peru's chief urban settlement in the Amazon region, Iquitos, resembles the stuff of popular myth. Lost in the middle of the jungle on the banks of the Amazon itself, it is a faded monument to the vanished dreams of the rubber barons. In the town centre there are cobbled streets and earthenware imported from Portugal, and an iron house designed by Gustave Eiffel for the 1889 Great Exhibition in Paris and transported here by a rubber baron. Around this splendid, if decaying centre, however, spreads the floating shanty town of Belén, which is the heart of the river trade.

Many of the houses here are built on rafts: life on board appears colourful as canoes stocked with forest produce come and go, but the population of 300,000 is desperately poor, and exposed to diseases such as cholera. Here, the population consists mainly of *mestizos* drawn to the town by successive booms, drug traffickers and, more recently, oil prospectors.

Located more than 2000 miles from the Amazon's mouth, the river is nevertheless almost a mile wide at Iquitos. At the end of the 19th century, when the city generated huge wealth, people from Lima were

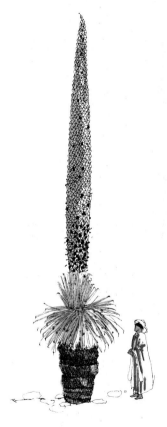

The Puya raimondii *is a bromeliacea which grows on the Andean plateaus and often reaches a height of some 20 feet. Birds seek refuge on the plants but sometimes become impaled on its spikes.*

prepared to travel by sea around Cape Horn and then all the way up the Amazon from Brazil. This was the era when rubber barons shipped their mineral water from Vichy, and their dirty laundry was washed in Paris. More than one street fountain was built to flow with champagne. In the Malecón district relics of these former extravagances are still visible: crumbling houses with ceramic tiles and corroded ironware. Eiffel's Iron House also rusts in the scalding sunshine close to the central Plaza de Armas. The docks at Iquitos still bustle with activity, as forest products, animals, fish or turtles, are brought in to market. From Iquitos boats travel downstream toward Leticia and the common border with Brazil and Colombia.

Pucallpa and Iquitos are good examples of the environmental destruction of the Amazon, juxtaposing modern materialistic society with the remaining fragments of an ancient culture eroded to the point of extinction. There is only one glimmer of hope in the *selva alta*. In the district of San Martín, a community flourishes, where Andeans and Amazonians live in harmony. The local dialect combines Quechua and an assortment of Amazon dialects, and the festivals, dance, cookery and costume combine the best of both worlds.

Andean dwellings are often built of adobe and comprise several buildings, a home and a few annexes. In the background are some eucalyptus trees which were introduced to Peru from Australia.

Where the conquerors landed

Upstream of Iquitos, the river Marañón winds its way westwards to the *cordillera,* and then south to Cajamarca. The journey across the Andes to Peru's northern coast is a comparatively simple affair. Here, the mountains are lower and the roads less tortuous. In the valleys, the climate is tropical, but above them, the hillsides are blanketed with conifers – a rare sight in the Andes. The lowest regions of all are rich enough, and receive sufficient rain, to support paddy fields. On the coast lies Piura, Peru's most northerly town. Founded

by Pizarro in 1532, it is close to the spot where the first *conquistadores* landed. Today it is Peru's sixth largest city, and a centre of rice cultivation.

Rice plays an important part in the Peruvian diet. In pre-Columbian times, the people had four staples: maize and potatoes on the coast, cassava in the Andes, and bananas in the Amazon. Rice arrived much later with Chinese coolies and Japanese labourers in the 19th century, and it too has become popular. These five foodstuffs now constitute the basis of the Peruvian diet, although the extent to which they are used varies according to the season. Other popular ingredients include fresh-water and sea fish, guinea pig, sheep and other animals, fruits, roots, leaves and herbs – cooked with skills refined over thousands of years, and more recently elaborated by the influence of European, Asian and African cuisine.

The demand for rice in Peru is now such that parts of the northern coast have been converted to paddy fields, which are watered by wells, modern irrigation systems or by the great Indian hydraulic system. Alongside the rice paddies are gigantic sugar-cane plantations, fields of cotton and smaller orchards of mango, banana and citrus fruits.

The north coast's other great contribution to the Peruvian table is fish. Once the world's largest supplier of fish, Peru has become a victim of climatic change caused by the Niño current of warmer water, which has driven away many of the species dependent on the cold, nutrient-rich waters from Antarctica. Since the earliest times, people on the Pacific coast made their living from the sea. Pre-Columbian farmers even used fish to fertilise their crops. During the 19th century, Europeans discovered guano – the excrement of the seagull – to be one of the richest soil nutrients in the world. And later still, they introduced methods of turning fish – notably the *anchoveta* – into meal and oil for cattle feed. Peru

Even today, the production of adobe bricks is entirely manual. The land is dug, turned to mud and set into blocks which are then left to bake in the sun.

soon became the world's leading manufacturer and exporter of fish by-products. Ports north of Lima, such as Chimbote, benefited from the boom in guano. These places took on the characteristics of frontier towns, as people flooded there to exploit their rich, if smelly, treasure. A lot of people made themselves very rich, but their greed eventually backfired. Stocks of *anchoveta* were wiped out through over-fishing and the industry died.

The whole of the long northern coast is now devoted to agriculture and trade. Fields have also been reclaimed from the San Lorenzo desert. It is the members of these farming communities – not inhabitants of a character-less modern city – who give the area its distinctive character.

Since the introduction of agrarian reforms during the leftist military governments of the 1960s, the white Creole culture which once dominated the region has almost vanished. Deprived of their *haciendas*, the high-society families of Spanish descent have dispersed. But

their influence can still be felt: in a dance called the *tondero*, for example, or in *natilla,* a delicacy consisting of cream flavoured with carob.

Sipán, around 15 miles south of Chiclayo, is the site of two extraordinary tombs dating from the time of the Moche people who flourished until around AD 700. The tombs were preserved by the dry desert and remained undisturbed by grave-robbers until 1987. The find was crucial to pre-Columbian archaeologists, allowing them a first glimpse at the Moche people's skills in metallurgy. The tombs contained gold, silver, and jewelled ornaments of fantastic quantity. Many of the finds, as well as artefacts from the cultures of Peru's northern coastal valleys, are displayed at the Bruning Museum in Lambayeque, close to Chiclayo. The Sipán tombs contained the remains of warrior-priests now known as *el Señor de Sipán* ('the gentleman of Sipán') and *el Viejo Señor de Sipán* ('the old gentleman of Sipán'). As well as the structure that contained these tombs is the Huaca Rajada, a fine example of an adobe brick temple with its irregular stepped terracing. Two larger structures were dedicated to the sun gods and the Moon gods. Pottery finds indicate that buildings and vessels alike were painted with scenes from mythology.

Mountain stronghold

Cajamarca, some 9000 feet high in the Andes, was the site of Pizarro's extraordinary meeting in 1532 with the Inca Atahualpa. In pre-Columbian times, the balance of trade between the fertile valleys in the upper Andes and the coastal plain cities was fairly equitable, and alliances were established between the desert empire and the mountain kingdom.

Ever since Pizarro, though, the city has been cursed with one misfortune or another. Suprisingly, there is little to see in the way of Inca relics, but the city does feel traditionally Andean. The beauty of Cajamarca's large valley and its surrounding mountains is tarnished by the memory of centuries of cruel exploitation of the Indians by the *gamonales* (masters of the *haciendas*). Overpopulated and ravaged by droughts, the countryside around Cajamarca is, nevertheless, the main source of water for the plantations of the coast and much of the *selva alta.*

Cajamarca has produced many of Peru's great poets, writers, musicians, painters, politicians and intellectuals; its crafts include textiles, hats, pottery and stone-cutting, and the city's cuisine is considered to be the finest in Peru. It also has some fine examples of Spanish colonial

In the central cordillera, *the Indians decorate their gourds with intricate designs, representing both religious and secular scenes from rural life.*

In Cajamarca, the imposing carved stone porticos (opposite) *and wrought ironwork* (below) *are outward signs of a patrician household's wealth. They stand in stark contrast to the industrious traders in the streets outside.*

architecture in palaces such as the splendidly filigreed Palace of the Condes de Ucedo, though many of its churches have a strangely squat appearance – for a long time none of them had towers, to avoid paying a Spanish tax on finished religious buildings. One, the Church of San Francisco, houses a set of bones believed by many experts to be those of Atahualpa. Another reminder of the past is the annual Corpus Christi festival, which within living memory was led by senior members of the local Canachin family, claiming descent from pre-Inca chieftains.

Over the millennia since the formation of civilisation in Peru, the Trujillo region has been the most prominent social, cultural and economic presence. Two of the great pre-Columbian societies were founded here: the Mochicas or Moche and the Chimú who dominated the region from AD 1000 until AD 1470. There are five major archaeological sites around Trujillo.

Chan Chan, the once great capital of the Chimú people and a remarkable adobe structure, was conquered by the Incas. From construction to decline, its life probably spanned no more than 150 years. Each successive ruler appears to have built himself a new palace and turned that of his predecessor into a mausoleum. Today little more than the mud walls of ten royal compounds remain, though they give visitors an idea of the grand scale of construction. There were probably more than 10,000 houses on this 6.5-square-mile site and, before the Spanish looted them, many funerary mounds containing considerable wealth. Wells, reservoirs and food storehouses, can all be identified. So wealthy were the Chimú that their mud walls were decorated with precious metals. The motifs include birds or fish, humans, waves and zigzag patterns. Though the ruins were damaged by freak rains, the decorative friezes have been preserved. Each of the palaces at Chan Chan had its ceremonial courts, royal apartments, and cemetery hidden behind mud walls. The graves held gold and silver and black ceramic work.

The Huaca Arco Iris (Rainbow Temple) lies so close to Trujillo that it is now situated in a suburb. This heavily ornamented, square building was uncovered

Under an acid-green dais rests a small coffin, painted white to symbolise the innocence of a dead child. In rural areas, where poverty is extreme, infant mortality is commonplace.

only in 1903; it is well preserved, and many of the decorative motifs have been restored. It was probably Chan Chan's main temple, although the thick defensive walls and single entrance suggest a military significance. Huaca Esmeralda, a temple situated between Trujillo and Chan Chan, has a number of friezes with similar motifs: sea-birds and animals, waves and fishing themes.

The Huaca del Sol and the Huaca de la Luna, Temples of Sun and Moon, are two massive adobe structures just to the south of Trujillo. Severely eroded by time, by Spanish colonial vandalism and generations of grave-robbers, the complete structure was probably

In Cajamarca, ponchos are usually dark red; as is the case throughout the Andes, people do not go out bareheaded. On market days, peasants from the whole region crowd the streets and squares.

Set against a background of Spanish tiles, a peasant couple wait in Cajamarca, daunted by the size of the city.

once over 140 feet high. The scale of its base suggests that it must have compared with Europe's largest cathedrals; to build it almost 150 million adobe bricks were used. The Sun Temple and the smaller Moon Temple – situated across a windswept plaza – probably predate Chan Chan by several hundred years.

Huanchaco, a fishing village on the coast just north of Trujillo, is a delightful alternative to the dusty pyramids and also provides a glimpse of pre-Columbian history. Here the fishermen still use *totora* reed boats or rafts with turned-up prows almost identical to those in the ancient Chan Chan friezes.

It was along this coast that colonial *haciendas*, irrigated by the old Mochica water channels, flourished and, with them, the splendid Creole culture of their owners. Trujillo devoted itself to the most sophisticated of the Creole pleasures: Peruvian stepping horses, coquettish *marinara* dances, exquisite seafood dishes, hospitality, architecture and elegant dress.

The Creole culture survived until the early 1970s, when the great *haciendas* were expropriated and the suave men and their fine ladies were dispersed to Lima or abroad. Their land was inherited by the descendants of the slaves and *peones* – the blacks from Africa, the Asian labourers and the Indians from the Andes. The workers now have money and land, but acquiring them doomed Creole culture.

The modern city of Trujillo, founded by Pizarro himself in 1536 and once a centre of colonial and Creole art, has become an industrial centre and, with a population of 750,000, it is now northern Peru's principal city. Some of Trujillo's great houses are decaying but the Plaza de Armas is as well preserved as that in any Peruvian city. Trujillo also has the advantage of one of the most pleasant climates in coastal Peru – dry, warm (but not too hot) and none of the fogs that afflict the capital Lima.

Chimbote lies farther south along the coast, between Trujillo and Lima. The land surrounding Chimbote is now a desert, its aridity exacerbated by the clearance of the *lomas* (bush vegetation) and the deforestation of the eastern Andes. Peasants trying to scratch a living here are now forced to bring in water from farther afield. Along with several other areas, the region is constantly lobbying the government to divert rivers whose normal course carries them to the Amazon or the Atlantic. The people of the Andes, who for centuries were suppliers of food to the coast, are now being asked to slake the thirst of the coast as well; and each large coastal town has to secure an Andean 'reserve supply' to ensure its survival.

Roots of Andean civilisation

Huaraz lies at the heart of Peru's most exciting region. Two and a half thousand years before the arrival of Pizarro, the first pan-Andean civilisation evolved in Chavín de Huantar: a culture characterised by its astonishing architecture of galleries and underground passages, by the terrifying ways in which it portrayed its gods, and by the establishment of trade routes between the Andes and the coast and the Amazon.

Originating around 900 BC, Chavín art was the first true Andean art style and Peru's oldest identifiable culture. At the temple, honeycombed underground passages lead to the carving of a feline monster from whose body spring small heads of snakes. This is the creator-God of the Chavín peoples, whose worship was the basis of their culture. Other animals – eagles, condors, jaguars and crocodiles – decorate the stone. Gruesome figures, apparently warriors, hold the severed heads of their enemies.

Although several kingdoms and cultures rose and fell after Chavín, the Spanish were astonished by the opulence and beauty of the region. They established large workshops here, using skilled Indian craftsmen, whose crafts flourish to this day. Much of their output is gobbled up by tourists, but their embroidery decorates their clothes at festival time.

Festivals are an integral part of Peruvian folklore

The Humboldt Current, which sweeps up from the Antarctic, is responsible for the aridity of Peru's Pacific coast. But it compensates for this by bringing abundant fish stocks.

These boats, made of bundles of reeds, are called caballitos *by the fishermen of the north coast. They are similar in design and construction to the* totoras *of Lake Titicaca.*

around the Huaraz area. The warm-up for a feast day can start a week before the event, with the arrival of the musicians. Each member of the community is assigned a role in the preparation of masses, processions, feasts, games and dances. The festival lasts from two days before the saint's day until a day after. The festivities often include bullfights or re-enactments of the battle between the Inca Atahualpa and Francisco Pizarro, the discovery of America, or dramatic episodes in earlier Inca history. The feasts feature spiced ham, guinea pig, and vegetable stews cooked for days in large earthenware pots.

Huaraz is visually stunning, with its panorama of snow-covered peaks rising to almost 22,000 feet above sea level. One of the most amazing features of this landscape is that it is only a few miles, as the crow flies, from the tropical palms and fruit trees that shelter in the inter-Andean corridor.

These contrasts are due to the comparative youth of the Andes which also gives rise to regular upheavals. In 1970 a vast slab of the Huascarán crashed down, demolishing small towns and villages in its way. Earthquakes are a fact of life here; they feature frequently in Indian ritual and legend and are treated with something approaching nonchalance. Within days of a quake, mountain slopes will once again be swarming with oxen, ploughing between the mighty blocks of stone scattered by the avalanche.

The valley of Mantaro, which stretches between Jauja and Huancayo, is filled with the colour and fragrance of eucalyptus, a welcome oasis after the pale yellow grasslands of the plateau above. The Indians here, who are descendants of the valiant Huancas, still follow the old craft traditions, producing beautiful carpets, coloured with natural vegetable dyes, and gourds engraved with agricultural and ceremonial scenes. By

You cannot help being impressed by the skill and daring of the men who take such flimsy craft as these caballitos *into the open sea.*

contrast, Huancayo, with its drab cosmopolitan architecture and its emphasis on commerce, lacks charm and splendour.

The journey to Lima is breathtaking. The barrier of the Andes at this point is formidable, and visitors are struck by the natural beauty and by the feats of engineering required to cut a road and lay tracks for the little train which climbs more than 15,000 feet.

This cheerful woman is preparing one of Peru's most popular anticuchos *(delicacies):* ox hearts barbecued and served with potatoes and a hot sauce.

Lima: City of Kings

When Francisco Pizarro founded Lima he called it the City of Kings. But the Spanish soon adopted the Indian name Rímac, after the shallow river running through it. Lima was simply a corruption of the river's name.

Sited between the Andes and the Pacific Ocean, latter-day Lima has spread to the coast and now

connects with the old port, Callao. Legend claims that, when he created his capital at the mouth of the Río Rímac, Francisco Pizarro was the victim of a magic spell, worked by Indians. For there is no other spot on the Peruvian coast that is so constantly shrouded in sea-mist. Not content with robbing the inhabitants of sun, the climate denied them rain, too. The peculiarities of the Pacific's Humboldt Current mean that Limeños can live without a roof if they choose, for they will never get wet. Instead, they exist for much of the year under a grey *garúa* sky, which blots out both the sun and any refreshing rain.

The flat roofs of some middle-class homes have proved an ideal base for the next generation to construct its own dwelling on top – with a flat roof on top just in

case the grandchildren also need to build a future home.

Lima's rapid growth and job market have spawned huge shanty towns (*barriadas*), and parts of the old city centre have become a vast open market where huge numbers live on filth-strewn pavements.

Fleeing from rural poverty, these peasants have flooded into the old city, yet they still try to maintain links with their roots by forming regional associations, celebrating traditional festivals and travelling home regularly. But the children of immigrants feel no such link with the past. For them the prospects are bleak. Unemployment is very high and most of them will have to eke out a living by hawking or petty crime. The result

is a spectacular crime rate. To make matters worse, exhaust from motor traffic combines with the sea-fog to produce chronic pollution.

Despite these shortcomings, the city has many redeeming features. It gives the impression of being a charming provincial town. This is partly due to its architecture: large colonial houses, with patios and wooden balconies, on well-organised narrow streets, each of which bears an ancient name derived from the occupation of its erstwhile inhabitants. There are also a number of unspoiled corners of the past, such as the old centre (*cercado*).

Lima inhabitants love wit: irony and wordplay are the currency of conversation and both are repaid with an appreciative laugh or smile. The people like the good life, gathering round a guitar player (*cajón*) to sing or dance the Peruvian waltz, the national *marinera*, the *tondero* of the north or the Afro-Peruvian *landó*. The people of Lima show great hospitality to foreigners – but little to provincial Peruvians – and the principle of

In the centre of Lima, there are still many old colonial buildings, characterised by the Moorish design of their balconies.

Poverty has caused the proliferation of small, marginal occupations, such as these shoe-blacks who do a brisk trade in the towns and cities.

sharing (in the passing round of a single glass, for example) is much valued.

Courtship has been raised to an art form in Lima. The flirtatiousness of Lima's women has long been famous: old engravings show *tapadas*, women who hide their faces behind veils and occasionally flash a seductive glance. The play of looks, the use of love letters, *piropos* (gallant remarks), and the romantic rendezvous all have their place in the highly organised ritual. But it is not a game to be played by the uninitiated.

Pizarro laid out his city in 1535 around the central square or Plaza de Armas. It survives even though the city was twice almost entirely destroyed and rebuilt after earthquakes in 1646 and 1687. Lima enjoyed special status as the capital of Spain's New World until the early 19th century. For much of this period it was one of the world's most prosperous cities.

Lima has been unlucky with its cathedral: the first was begun beside the Plaza de Armas in 1555 but was replaced by a second in 1625. The new building was destroyed by the 1746 earthquake and what exists today is a reconstruction. For generations, Peruvians had gazed upon mummified remains in the cathedral that they believed to be Pizarro's – he died in Lima in 1541, just nine years after he first landed in the Inca realms. However, a second skull was found in the crypt in 1977, and seven years later experts identified as that of the old *conquistador*. Other remains can be seen in the catacombs of the San Francisco monastery, where tens of thousands of skeletons are grimly arranged. The Museum of the Inquisition, where waxwork unfortunates still agonise under torture, and the Santo Domingo convent, which contains the tomb of Santa Rosas, the New World's first saint, complete a tour of Lima's religious sites.

What the Spanish really came for was the gold, some of which is on view at the Museo de Oro del Perú (Museum of Peruvian Gold). Like Colombia's gold museum, this is a massive bank vault which, along with a superb collection of armaments, contains the best collection of pre-Columbian artefacts in South America. These include necklaces, bracelets and funerary items, many encrusted with gems, from both Inca and pre-Inca cultures. Archaeological remains can also be seen in several other museums, and the privately owned Amano Museum contains one of the world's finest collections of ancient textiles, including those of the pre-Inca Paracas and Chancay cultures.

A century ago, a commercial centre was built at Miraflores, taking some of the pressure away from the old centre. Then, as the middle classes moved in, the upper classes moved to the suburbs, where they built themselves estates of American-style ranch houses served by their own shopping centres. A single road in Miraflores bears witness to the changing face of city life in Peru. At one end of the street are large adobe houses, built at the beginning of the century to accommodate extended families; farther down are villas, constructed 40 years later for the three-generation family of grandparents, parents and children; farther still and you find blocks of flats, designed specifically for today's nuclear family.

The dry earth of the desert has preserved the best evidence of Peru's glorious past. Finds include the naturally mummified corpses of ancient dignitaries, clad in their funeral finery.

Venezuela

The first European explorers of South America hoped to find
the legendary gold mines of El Dorado in modern Venezuela.
Later generations found the real 'black gold' of oil. Venezuela
gave South America its Great Liberator, Simón Bolívar,
who led the fight against Spanish colonialism.
Today, falling oil revenues have left it struggling with massive
international debts and distressing contrasts of wealth and poverty.
But none of that thas quenched the exuberance of the people and
their love of every kind of festival.

A typical Andean village, in the state of Merida; the single street is lined with closely packed, squat houses, their thick walls made of earth and then whitewashed or daubed with pinkish clay. Donkeys, mules and Andean ponies are the only transport. The high, narrow pavements double as river banks when the rains transform the road into a furious torrent.

Previous page: A Venezuelan from the Merida region walks for hours along the stony paths of the Andes to the town where he will sell the contents of his bundle: a few vegetables grown on his rancho, eggs, mangos, avocados and pawpaws.

The Little Venice of the Caribbean

When Christopher Columbus dropped anchor in the Orinoco river delta in 1498, his crew asked him where they were: 'In Paradise,' he replied. Amerigo Vespucci, the Italian adventurer who would later give his name to the whole of the newly discovered American continent, thought differently.

The brackish waters, voracious insects and intense heat of Lake Maracaibo, a vast Caribbean lagoon, made him liken the country to an inferno. But the sight of straw huts built on stilts over the water and Indians plying between them in their dugout canoes also reminded him of home. So he named the land 'Little Venice' or 'Venezuela'.

Vespucci and his comrades came in search of fabled gold mines, and though it took different forms through the centuries, the same hunt for these elusive riches plagues the continent even today. The drama did not end when the legend of *El Dorado* was in large part fulfilled by the discovery of the 'black gold' under Maracaibo, that for a time made Venezuela the world's third largest oil exporter. Oil has indeed brought wealth to Venezuela, but the wealth is mixed with poverty, and it has also brought discord. Add to that the tradition of political activism that began when a Venezuelan, Simón Bolívar, first broke the hold of the Spanish empire in 1811, and it is little wonder the country's history has been a turbulent one.

The crystal mountain

Stretching from the Caribbean southwards to the watershed of the Amazon river, Venezuela's 220,000 square miles are roughly divided into mountains, plains and tropical forests, and are cut in two by the mighty Orinoco river – the continent's second longest at 1600 miles. The country has no shortage of natural attractions, from the massive wall of the Coastal *cordillera* – the tail end of the Andes – to sights such as Angel Falls in the Guiana Highlands, where the Churún river drops 2640 feet, making it the world's highest waterfall. This is a region of geologically ancient formations such as Mount Roraima, the inspiration for Sir Arthur Conan Doyle's tale of jungle exploration and mystery, *The Lost World.*

The first discoverers to follow in the wake of Columbus cared little for such sights. Rather than exult in the purity of the New World, they defiled it with the greed and rivalry they brought from the Old World: greed for the gold they were convinced they would find once the city of *El Dorado* was discovered; and rivalry between the empires of Spain and Britain.

Though later stories located him in Colombia, it was in Venezuela that the hunt began for a mythical chieftain who smothered himself in pitch and then rolled in gold dust before diving into a lake, while Indians on the shore cast their jewels and gold ornaments after him as an offering to the gods. The hunt was started by the Spanish around 1530, but the most famous explorer to become infected by the legend of *El Dorado* was the Englishman Sir Walter Raleigh.

He found nothing on his two expeditions into the Venezuelan interior in 1595 and 1617 – a failure which ultimately cost him his head. As he awaited execution in the Tower of London, Raleigh stubbornly pursued his dream, writing of a 'large, rich and beautiful empire' that would one day be carved from the magical forest, at whose heart was a 'mountaine of christall' that he believed he had seen while travelling years before with Indians on the Orinoco.

There was, of course, no crystal mountain, and after Raleigh's countrymen had been pushed back to the neighbouring island of Trinidad, Venezuela settled down to a sleepier existence as a backwater of the

Cattleya mossiae, *known as the* Flor de Mayo *(Mayflower), is one of hundreds of varieties of orchid to grow in Venezuela, but the only one to be chosen as a national emblem. The* cattleya *motif is also worn as jewellery, fashioned in solid gold and set with fine pearls from the island of Margarita.*

At an altitude of some 10,000 feet, the small town of Mucuchies (opposite) *is the highest in the country. Its doors and narrow windows are kept constantly closed against the chill air.*

Opposite: *Marabouts, red ibis and snowy white egrets line the banks of one of the innumerable rivers that cross the plains of the state of Apure. Named after its principal river, which is second in Venezuela only to the Orinoco, the state forms a gigantic bird reserve for many remarkable species.*

Spanish empire – that is, when Dutch pirates were not attacking the pearl fisheries or trading illegally in salt, tobacco, cocoa and other commodities. The Spanish had, after all, been the first to establish settlements back in 1523 on the coast of Cumaná – to the east of the modern capital, Caracas – despite the presence of Arawak and Carib Indians.

In 1535 an expedition to Venezuela had been led by Germans who were granted rights to establish settlements in the northern part of the country by the Holy Roman Emperor, Charles V, whose vast realms included the Latin American territories of his maternal grandparents, Ferdinand and Isabella of Spain. In 1556, though, the Spanish regained the region, and kept it until 1821, when the insurgent army of Simón Bolívar defeated them decisively at Carabobo.

If Spain had not possessed other spectacular Latin dominions, it might have appreciated Venezuela more – for there is much to appreciate. To the north and west near the coast, the land rises to the *cordillera* with its sharp ridges, dark, lush valleys and snow-capped mountains, their peaks sometimes lost in the clouds. The Venezuelan Andes stretch from the Colombian border north-eastwards for 200 miles. These are the *paramos,* 12,000-foot high terraces and plateaus. The Cordillera del Norte runs east-west for 600 miles in two parallel branches, while three heavily populated and fertile valleys run between them.

Humid mangrove swamps stretch from the shore to the thickly wooded base of this mountain wall, their hanging roots sheltering a plethora of animal life. From the sweltering heat of Lake Maracaibo, now bristling with oil derricks, it is less than 100 miles to the frozen mountains where even the hardiest wear furs.

South of the mountain regions lies the heartland of Venezuela: the *llanos* (plains) of savannah and scrub forest. The *llanos,* several hundred square miles of

For several miles around the town of Canaima, the Carrao river, a tributary of the Caroni crashes through rapids and down cataracts. In the middle of the impenetrable forest, the thunder of millions of tons of water explodes like an overture to the Apocalypse.

Heaven or Hell? A brief, but, splendid sunset silhouettes the forest of oil derricks which rises from the salt waters of the vast Lake Maracaibo. Seen from the air, the thousands of metal frames, set at 1000-foot intervals, show a perfect symmetry.

For these two workmen at Lagunillas, one of the oil-fields on the east coast of Lake Maracaibo, air-conditioning, modern technology and high salaries ease the discomforts of daily life in a torrid climate. Venezuela has 50,000 people employed in the extraction, transport and refining of this 'black gold'.

vast area of more than 385,000 square miles. This includes tropical rain forests, the *llanos* of both Colombia and Venezuela, and the Guiana Highlands. The upper and lower reaches of the river are separated by cataracts at Atures and Miapures.

Though the Orinoco was first sighted by Columbus in 1498, the Spanish adventurer Lope de Aguirre first travelled most of its length in 1560 as part of Pedro de Ursúa's ill-fated expedition to find *El Dorado* in the Amazon headwaters. The German naturalist Alexander von Humboldt was one of the first to explore its upper reaches in 1799 and discovered the Casiquiare river which connects the Orinoco to the Río Negro, which is a tributary of the Amazon. It was not until 1951, however, that the source of the river was actually located.

To the south of the river, the grasslands of the *llanos* give way to the forest, mountains and plateaus of Guiana, covered by a tangle of dense tropical rain forest that eventually blends with the larger Amazon forest. Venezuela has a wide variety of animal life, including monkeys, jaguars, pumas, sloths, anteaters, armadillos, the strange bristly pig-like creatures known as peccaries and, in its coastal waters, the ungainly sea mammals, manatees. Tropical birds, such as parrots and macaws, are abundant.

In the southern region of El Callao, too, are the gold-diggings, where thousands of miners dig through the mud for riches that, once found, will soon be spent in the bars and bordellos of shoddy boomtowns.

Venezuelans still talk about the independent state of Guyana as though it were their own territory – as part of

'Ayer salio la lancha Nueva Esparta!' - 'Yesterday, the New Sparta was launched!' On the island of Margarita, which is famous for its pearls, the story is chanted, mimed and danced in time to the maracas. A fisherman on his wheeled boat leads the procession through the streets of the town.

desolate near-emptiness, are scorched by sun for six months of the year, and flooded for the other six by the muddy waters of the Orinoco. Here, on the patchy seasonal grass, herds of cattle graze, until the floods force them to take refuge in the foothills of the Andes. This region, which covers almost a third of the country, is largely treeless but rich in bird life. Beside the rivers, too, can be found crocodiles and the capybara, a huge, partly aquatic rodent, which can grow as much as four feet long.

The giant Orinoco river cuts right through the centre of these *llanos*, flowing lazily east from its source in the Venezuelan and Colombian Andes towards the Atlantic Ocean. It enters this via a large delta covering about 7800 square miles. The river discharges its pale-brown silt far out into the ocean, black with muddy slime, flecked with uprooted greenery. The Orinoco drains a it once was. In the last century, a quarrel between Venezuela and Britain over this gold-rich territory prompted intervention by the United States, which in 1895 persuaded Britain to submit to the findings of an international tribunal. In the event, the tribunal came down largely on Britain's side.

Extremely old rock formations, such as Mount Roraima, absorb huge amounts of water that cascade down their perpendicular walls as waterfalls. Angel Falls, discovered in 1935 by James Angel, a US explorer and aviator, is the world's highest cataract. It is in this region that Indian groups, notably the Yanomami, are to be found, living, to a large extent as their ancestors did long before Europeans arrived in the Americas. Venezuela was one of the last countries to be extensively populated, and there are still blank areas on the map.

The landscape of Venezuela is forbidding, but it is also enormously rich. Below its unstable surface, occasionally disturbed by the rumbling of earthquakes, lies a vast mineral wealth – gold, silver, bauxite and diamonds. Above all, Venezuela is one of the world's largest petroleum producers, with proven reserves of about 58.1 billion barrels including the rich heavy-oil belt in the Orinoco basin. Since drilling began in 1913, Venezuela's economy has been built upon oil. It is the nationalised oil industry that provides 80 per cent of export revenues and that sustains the country's two main political parties with powers of patronage; and it is oil that pays for the health and education services. Oil, too, is to blame for the foreign debt of $34 billion, which was run up in the expectation that ever-rising revenues would pay all the bills. They have not.

Venezuelan peasant women carry their loads on their heads. Resting on a flat, round cushion, a basket of bricks or an old paraffin can filled with reddish water may be transported many miles. The men, on the other hand, carry their loads on their backs or use donkeys.

The Venezuelan capital of Caracas, with its luxurious tower blocks and monumental tree-lined avenues, is beginning to fill the valley in which it lies and to encroach on the virgin forest. Here, intrepid workmen are being hauled up the scaffolding of one of the many high-rise buildings currently under construction.

Hopes of fame and fortune

Throughout the 16th and 17th centuries, the winds blowing across the Atlantic towards the Caribbean swept many a poverty-stricken gentleman from his native Andalusia in southern Spain towards La Guaira, the port of entry to a new country and, these adventurers hoped, towards a new fortune.

The allure of Venezuela's legendary wealth was as great for the Spanish as it was for Sir Walter Raleigh: they came here in droves with beasts and baggage. Even today, La Guaira is still Venezuela's major commercial sea-port, though most of the country's minerals and oil are exported by other specialised ports, such as Maracaibo, Tucacas and Punta Carbón. But La Guaira is still stretched to capacity – and beyond. Ninety per cent of the goods imported into Venezuela are landed at this one port. In addition, cruise ships regularly dock in the harbour, their upper decks towering above the forest of cranes.

Today, of course, most visitors reach Venezuela by air. But they too must start down on the shoreline. This coastal plain, all but non-existent in places, is so narrow that passengers arriving by air are bound to wonder where on earth they are going to land. When the runway finally comes into view, it is nothing more than a rectangular patch reaching out into the sea.

The aeroplane door opens on to a furnace of white, hot light. Crowds jostle, and people utter cries of joy, recognition and welcome – all against the constant hubbub of *maracas* (hollow gourds with pebbles or dried beans inside), guitars and transistor radios. In the airport, as everywhere else, music is the Venezuelans' constant companion, blasting from bars, taxis and private cars. Out on the street, the honking car horns compete with the cries of ice-cream vendors and of those selling *chicha* (a thick, white, maize-based drink) or *guarapo* (a slightly fizzy, brown drink extracted from sugar-cane). You have arrived.

'Caracas! Caracas!' chant the taxi drivers of La Guaira, as they lean against their huge American cars. The journey to the capital city takes the visitor more than 3000 feet up into the mountains. Protected by steep precipices and hidden by dense forest, Caracas was once virtually inaccessible. It was not until the beginning of this century that a proper road, linking the capital to the coast, was blasted into the flank of the mountain. As recently as 40 years ago, the dizzy twists on this road were still so dangerous that there were armed police in look-out boxes at every one of its 400 bends. In the late 1950s, an eight-lane motorway from the coast to Caracas was constructed by French engineers and the journey to the capital now takes only 10 minutes.

Nestling in an immense valley, stretching out along the Guaire river, Caracas enjoys one of the world's best climates, with an average temperature of 24°C (75°F).

The Simón Bolívar Tower (above) is one example of the modern architecture that characterises much of present-day Caracas. The city's colonial past survives, however, in this square (below) with its old-fashioned lamps and its equestrian statue honouring the Liberator himself, Simón Bolívar.

Even in the rainy season, which runs from June through to October, heavy showers are almost always interspersed by spells of brilliant sunshine.

Despite its spectacular location, Caracas is not a beautiful place by any stretch of the imagination. For its critics, the city combines the worst of both the Americas – a graceless urban sprawl of freeways and skyscrapers, without the visual comfort of Hispanic architecture that enlivens other Latin cities. Despite the modernity there is dirt and decay aplenty, and the shanty-towns that make up two-thirds of the city are all the more jarring for their proximity to the gracious but fortified suburbs of the rich. Slums and shanties reach upwards, curling around the valleys and mountains in the race to occupy the available space.

Caracas, like other Latin cities, shows the dramatic colour contrasts of wealth and poverty: the jewel-like turquoise of swimming pools counterpoints the rusty-red hills covered with the battered tin roofs of the slum-dwellers.

Today over 80 per cent of Venezuela's 19 million people are city-dwellers (the capital has over 3 million inhabitants). In addition to the overcrowding, crime and rapidly worsening public services are the legacy of Venezuela's profligate spending of oil revenues. And the inhabitants of Caracas must now contend with worsening levels of industrial pollution.

There is little left of the city's long colonial past. The old, red-tiled buildings of the once-compact Spanish city, surrounded by sugar-cane plantations, have either succumbed to earthquakes – including one particularly destructive one at the beginning of this century – or to the equally destructive bulldozers of President Pérez Jiménez in the 1950s. In the course of his presidency, Pérez Jiménez reduced what was left of the old town to rubble. He demolished the colourful colonial streets with their high, narrow pavements, and replaced them with great expanses of marble, cement and reinforced concrete, bordered with grass lawns and luxury apartment blocks.

If the charm has been swept away, there has been an attempt to replace it with modern-day grandeur, and on the surface, at least, the city still offers all the trappings of affluence – skyscrapers, neon-lit streets, motorways and an efficient subway system. During the 1970s, billions were spent on providing the very best that petrodollars could buy in terms of architecture and services. The modern architecture is often striking and innovative: for example, the Centro-Banaven, a startling black, glass cube, and the 56-storey twin towers of the massive Parque Central complex – a city within the city. Great artists and craftsmen have been commissioned to produce sculpture and stained glass for the city's buildings, including Ferdinand Leger, Jean Arp and Henry Laurens.

None the less, most visitors view Caracas with a certain sadness, for the proliferation of the new cannot atone for the loss of the old. It is not just the newness and the sameness of the skyscrapers that daunts the visitor, it is the culture that inhabits them. Venezuela has embraced bureaucracy with dismal fervour, and many an exasperated traveller seeking a permit or pass from one of the ministries has wondered whether he will ever escape before being worn down by the Kafka-esque experience.

Yet fragments of the older charm of Caracas do survive. At the city's very centre stands the shady square with its statue of the Liberator, Simón Bolívar. Here stand the Panteón, where he is buried; the site marked by a brick copy of the little house where he was born; and the trees near the San Francisco church from under which he is said to have addressed the people.

The Great Liberator

Simón Bolívar lends more than his name to the national currency: it was he who created the sense of national identity and came tantalisingly close to forging an independent Hispanic federation that could have offered the continent an economic and political development similar to that in the United States.

The break-up of Spanish control began in 1806, when the revolutionary Francisco de Miranda, landed in Venezuela with a force recruited in the United States. Though he was easily repulsed by loyalist troops, Venezuela's revolutionary congress declared its independence from Spain on July 5, 1811. The stage was set for Bolívar the Liberator, the single most

Beauty, vivacity and elegance come naturally to the Caraqueños, *the people of Caracas. In well-to-do families, the* hembras (*girls*) *are cosseted and groomed in readiness for a life of leisure and luxury.*

Opposite: *By 9am, the temperature has usually risen to 30°C (85°F). Scores of street vendors sell ice-cream and cold drinks from their stalls in city squares, in front of offices and outside schools.*

important person in the struggle against Spanish authority.

Born in 1783, to a wealthy land-owning family in Caracas, Bolívar was influenced by Jean-Jacques Rousseau and other European thinkers, emerging as a leader of the revolutionaries in 1810. As the revolt's military leader, he was driven out by the Spanish but returned in 1813 to establish the second Venezuelan republic. Forced to flee to Jamaica in 1815, Bolívar later returned to the mainland by way of Colombia where he eventually achieved a major victory at the Battle of Boyacá.

He then created Gran Colombia, a federation of present-day Venezuela, Colombia, Panama and Ecuador, of which he became president. Bolívar linked up with the Argentine patriot José de San Martín in Ecuador, and proceeded south to Peru where he defeated the Spanish on a mountainside near Quito (now in Ecuador) in 1822. Together with the other South American revolutionaries, he drove the Spanish from the region in 1824. In 1828 Bolívar assumed dictatorial powers over the whole region but died just two years later, embittered and aware that his dream of liberal democracy would not flourish in South America. In 1830, Venezuela withdrew from Bolívar's Gran Colombia federation and became a sovereign state.

Where wealth divides

Bolívar's heirs and successors, the *Caraqueños,* are a mixed lot. Most people speak Spanish as their primary language and profess Roman Catholicism. About 67 per cent of the people are *mestizo* (mixed race), 21 per cent white, 10 per cent black, and 2 per cent Indian. What divides Venezuelans is not race but wealth: though its annual per capita income of over $3000 is the continent's highest and four times that in Bolivia, almost half Venezuela's 20 million people live in poverty. The culprit, perhaps, is oil. For though its revenues provide a third of the national income and three-quarters of the taxes, it employs just 1 per cent of the workforce. The results are plain for any visitor to see.

Down on the coast near La Guaira lies the small bay of Macuto, which has become popular as a tourist beach resort in recent years. Here, swimmers can bathe safely in waters that are protected by steel nets from the Caribbean's prolific shark population. Macuto is just one of a string of luxury resort beaches which have been developed along this stretch of coast. Now that the

A colonial house in Coro, the oldest town in all of South America. Thirty years ago, all of Venezuela's towns, including Caracas, were built entirely in this style.

shark problem has effectively been solved, they offer holiday-makers a veritable paradise – sandy beaches, swaying palm trees, clear blue water, an idyllic climate and superb hotels.

Yet just a few hundred yards inland from these resorts, you find a quite different Venezuela. Tucked behind the dream villas and the air-conditioned hotels are a jumble of shacks, built of cardboard boxes and roofed with corrugated iron and old car panels. Simmering in the heat, this shanty-town is home to some of the country's dispossessed. Half-starved, they live here with their dogs, hens and bristly black pigs. Heaven and Hell in Venezuela are within spitting distance of one another.

Though the urban population is centred in about 20 cities with more than 100,000 people, these contrasts

It may seem quiet beside the colonial houses in one of the few old streets in La Guaira; but everywhere else in the country's principal port, the streets are noisy and bustling.

are nowhere more evident than in Caracas. The quiet residential areas of La Castellana, Las Mercedes, and La Florida are far removed from the downtown glitz and flashing neon lights. Successful Venezuelan merchants live here, in fine houses (*quintas*) and in luxury villas with large tropical gardens, or in the magnificent apartment blocks on Altamira Square, their venetian blinds closed to the garishness of the business quarter.

On the perimeter of this rich city, however, disorderly agglomerations of shacks and *ranchitos* cling like pink leprous sores to the mountainsides, and each year they encroach farther into the forest. From all over Venezuela, men come to the capital in the hope of gleaning a few scraps of its wealth. They build their precarious dwellings in a day or two with whatever comes to hand, ready for their families to follow, usually with three or four hens, a pig or a goat – indeed, all their worldly possessions.

Perhaps more than any other country on this continent, Venezuela reflects the twin influences that have shaped it: the United States and Spain. This is a country of baseball, rodeos and cowboys. It is also a nation addicted to bullfights, *machismo* and other forms of display.

Wherever they might live, people rise early in Caracas. As soon as it begins to grow light, the bustle starts anew, accompanied by the habitual sound of music, car horns, shouts and laughter. The offices open around 8 o'clock, the schools at 8.30. By then, however, it is already over 30°C (85°F) and people hurry into air-conditioned buildings. Outside, in cars or vans, or pushing their small refrigerated carts of ice-cream and drinks, the street vendors collect at strategic points: school and college gates, the entrances to office blocks, or in the shade of the busy squares, such as El Silencio, La Candelaria and Bolívar. Here, too, the boot-blacks set to work, their clients reclining in chairs as they study the morning newspaper, perhaps *El Nacional* or *El Universal*.

The headlines are a guide to the country's sensational political life. There can be few countries, for instance, in which an attempted coup d'état is calmly followed by elections just a week later. In November 1992 at least

Swathed in their ample dresses, coloured scarves draped over their long, palm-oiled hair, Guajiro Indian women pile into ancient railway carriages for the journey from their village to a neighbouring market town in the state of Zulia.

At the market in Maracaibo, Guajiro Indians lay out their platanos verdes – enormous green bananas which, fried and salted, form a staple food throughout Venezuela. Other tropical fruits, including pineapples, guavas and mangos are also sold at the same market, along with fish and shellfish.

The national costume of this vast, ethnically diverse country is that of the llanero, the man of the plains. His liqui-liqui – a white, cotton suit with mandarin collar and patch pockets – is much favoured by high-society Venezuelan men, though they dispense with the straw hat, and wear shoes rather than alpargatas (sandals). The woman (llanera) wears a flounced, off-the-shoulder blouse, but the wide floral skirt is usually reserved for traditional celebrations.

170 people died when military officers tried to topple president Carlos Andrés Pérez, bringing to an end 35 years of democracy. It was not the first attempt. Only nine months earlier the same army officers had tried to overthrow the veteran politician. In 1989, just weeks after Pérez had taken office for the second time and announced an austerity programme soon after his champagne and lobster inauguration ceremony, over 300 people were shot dead in mass rioting to protest against cuts in subsidies for food, fuel and transport.

The difficulties encountered by Pérez are hardly new, for in the century up to 1958 democracy was little evident in Venezuela: a succession of dictatorships came to an end when the armed forces were virtually bought off with part of the oil revenues, though the agreement left the two ruling parties with a stranglehold on power and influence. After that, new civilian leaders such as Rómulo Betancourt, Raúl Leoni, Rafael Caldera, Luis Herrera Campins and Jaime Lusinchi made Venezuela an island of stability. Carlos Andrés Pérez, also president in the oil-rich era from 1974 to 1979, has found the 1990s an altogether tougher proposition as the country's economic prosperity dwindles: some estimates say oil would have to more than double in price for Venezuelans once again to enjoy the standard of living they had in the early 1980s.

Tomorrow's another day

Despite these troubles, Venezuelans are an exuberant people, their smiles and carefree movements demonstrating the sensual pleasure they derive from living in the present. Rich or poor, brown or white, they feel that life is there to be enjoyed; for many people this sentiment is spiced with the unshakeable belief that tomorrow will bring something even better. It is hardly surprising that 'tomorrow' – *mañana* – is one of the most used words in the Venezuelan vocabulary.

Newspapers, too, reflect their appetite for dramatic human-interest stories. Take this, for example: 'With one bite the man tore off her nose' (*'De un mordizco le arrancó la nariz'*); or, 'Awakening from his sleep under a tree, the lorry driver was surprised to find his leg being digested inside a giant snake, which, satiated, had fallen asleep'; or how about, 'Attacked by the Motilones [the country's only aggressive Indians], he kept his head, gathered up his severed arm and drove 125 miles to hospital where they sewed it back on'.

In such a divided society, one half loves to know how the luckier half lives. And what better way than through the gossip columns? Venezuelans are voracious consumers of the society pages. Here they might read of the 'coming out' party of some 15-year-old daughter of the elite. In high society (*sociedad*), these are extravagant affairs. Hundreds of guests gather in the gardens and on the patios of the great Andalusian-style villas. The emergent debutante, dressed like a film star, opens the dancing with her father and thereafter, if she is already engaged as is usually the case, she will be partnered by her *novio* (fiancé).

Alternatively, the featured event might just be a birthday party – though 'just' is hardly the word for these ostentatious events. Young Rafaela Ramírez, says the society column, has just celebrated her fifth birthday, and the picture shows a little girl smiling from

The llanero, *is a familiar figure in the* llanos (*plains*). *With his back straight, his head high and his eyes searching the distance, he keeps watch over his herds from the broad saddle of a pony.*

This llanero *has rounded up his scrawny cattle into the shade on a* hato (*cattle ranch*) *in the scorching state of Apure. It is the end of the dry season and the cattleman's main concern is to find enough water for those cattle bearing calves.*

Breaking in horses is one of the llanero's *main tasks. Like the Argentinian* gaucho *and the North American cowboy, he catches the animal with a lasso, leads it into the corral, and gradually tames and trains it. Rodeos, celebrating the* llanero's *skills are a popular form of entertainment in rural areas of Venezuela.*

a froth of ribbons and petticoats. She is brandishing the stick with which she has just demolished her *piñata*, a colourful crêpe-paper figure filled with little gifts which is hung from the ceiling and attacked by the young guests, who are then showered with toys and sweets.

The society columnist is unlikely, however, to venture into the poor districts or *barrios* where girls are often mothers at 12 or 13. Here, the baby's baptism is their one opportunity for ostentation. Like the society 'coming out', a baptism in the *barrio* is a time for the family to celebrate with as much show as possible.

Proximity to the shopping malls of Miami, the wealth which spews from underground and the Venezuelans' innate love of ostentation have all combined to produce a climate of conspicuous consumption. To their Spanish pride, the Venezuelans have added the North American passion for consumer durables. Thus, houses, gardens and luxury cars (as many as possible) represent essential status symbols for any successful Venezuelan. Most of the rich are of European descent. There are those who were drawn to Venezuela in the 1950s by President Pérez Jiménez' open-door policy; and there are those who can trace their roots back to Andalusian immigrants of the 16th century. The wealth came originally from sugar-cane, cocoa or coffee, but more recently they have diversified into property development, oil, mining and manufacturing.

Truly rich Venezuelan women are consummate shoppers. They descend on the cities of Europe and the United States, like visiting royalty, absorbing culture and consumer goods with equal relish. Back at home they spend their days in groups, cruising the shops, before retiring, exhausted, to their clubs. In Caracas these clubs correspond to subtle gradations of class and status. But the desire for ornamentation is not confined to the wealthy: in Caracas, bus and taxi drivers take enormous pride in their vehicles, decorating every space in the cab interior with religious artefacts, nosegays and assorted clinking ornaments.

Neither the sweltering heat nor the poverty appear to pose any impediment to being permanently well-

Laden with a harvest of fat green bananas (curats), this Waika Indian is returning from his conuco, *a tribal or family plantation created by burning the forests. When the soil is exhausted, a new plot of land will be burned, cleared and planted.*

The palm houses of the Guarao Indians are built on stilts above the Orinoco river. A row of curiaras *is moored below. These long, streamlined canoes, hollowed from the trunks of saman trees, are a tribute to the great skill of the Makiritares.*

preened; even the least well-off make sure that the national uniform of Latin America – a T-shirt and blue jeans – is immaculately clean and pressed. It would not be uncharitable to say that Venezuelan women are obsessed with their appearance. Whether they are going to work, to college or staying at home, they dress with infinite care. Make-up, hair, hats and jewellery are in place from first thing in the morning, and the Venezuelan woman always has a mirror at hand to check that they stay that way. Men are eager to play the flirting game. Taxi drivers oblige with lingering whistles or the classic male compliment – a shouted *Aie, chica!*

Cattle-raising on the plains

Not all Venezuelan life is played out in the jungle of asphalt and concrete, however: the country's true heartland is the *llanos,* the vast plains across which the

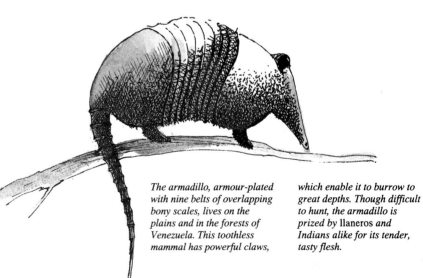

The armadillo, armour-plated with nine belts of overlapping bony scales, lives on the plains and in the forests of Venezuela. This toothless mammal has powerful claws, which enable it to burrow to great depths. Though difficult to hunt, the armadillo is prized by llaneros *and Indians alike for its tender, tasty flesh.*

cattlemen wandered. It was on the *llanero* people that Bolívar depended to drive out the Spanish, and today's Venezuelans still find their national identity in the figure of the *llanero*. Wearing his broad straw hat, his white *liqui-liqui* (an elegant suit with mandarin collar) and a pair of *alpargatas* (sandals) on his feet, this solitary hero can still be glimpsed crossing the plains, or winding along a mountain road, heading to some unknown destination astride a pony. Many of the urban poor are descendants of the *llanero,* who for centuries subsisted by taking on casual employment as cattle-handlers in exchange for a temporary roof and a loaf of corn bread. The people of the plains, on the other hand, are the descendants of the Indians – of the Quechuas and of the Caribs, who massacred the Quechuas in order to take their place; of the Guajiros, the pale-skinned tribes of the Andes; and of ebony-skinned Africans, brought here as slaves by the Spanish.

Not all the Indians have succumbed to the successive waves of migration from the Old World. In Venezuela, the term Indian is used to describe anyone with straight, black hair, high cheekbones and copper-coloured skin. Those who live in shacks on the outskirts of towns or in the concrete car parks of city tower blocks are generally referred to as urban Indians.

The Indians of the forest – the pure Indians – have no contact with those of the towns. They belong to one of three main groups: the Guaharibos, the Arawaks and the Caribs. As the Spanish colonists started to arrive, the Indians were pushed farther and farther into the hinterland of Venezuela. The smallest and weakest tribes were pushed the farthest and into the most inhospitable regions. It is for this reason that the Guaharibos and Waikas had the good fortune to end up in the inaccessible territory of the upper Orinoco, where they remain today, scattered into tiny groups.

To a foreign eye, these forest Indians are indeed primitive, leading a life that can have changed little since Columbus first stepped ashore half a millennium ago. They go naked except for the coloured designs painted on their skin and perhaps for a macaw feather or a piece of polished bamboo stuck through their ear or

the skin around their mouth. Their straight, black hair is basin-cut and they sometimes shave the tops of their heads to make a monk-like tonsure. The men hunt with bows and arrows or fish the waters of the Orinoco to feed themselves and their families.

Cities of the interior

Thanks to Venezuela's modern highway system, which is considered among the best in Latin America, and to its well-developed domestic air transport, travel to the

In the 'green hell' of its upper reaches, the Orinoco is fed by countless streams, rivers and lagoons. Several semi-nomadic tribes, belonging to the great families of Guaharibos, Waikas and Kakiritares, are scattered throughout this region. These fishermen, wearing Guaharibo ear ornaments and Western shorts, wade in closed ranks towards the bank of the lagoon, driving the fish before them.

This young Indian girl, from a tribe belonging to the Guaharibo family, is making a skirt from the thread of wild cotton, coloured with a charcoal and water dye. Like most Guaharibo women, she is wearing ear ornaments of natural cotton fibres, but her necklace of small, blue glass beads is typical of the Makiritares' costume.

This young woman, a member of the Guaharibo tribe, is wearing the bamboo face ornaments of the Waikas, and the ear decorations of her own people. The technique she is using to weave her deep basket originates with the Makiritares, proof of the constant exchanges between the different tribes.

country's interior presents few problems and there is much to see.

Ciudad Bolívar, located inland about 260 miles from the mouth of the Orinoco, was once named Angostura, and is the original home of the famous bitters. This cure, made from the crushed bark of a local tree mixed with honey, was invented by one of the town's doctors in 1824 and helped to free it of fever – later, in 1875, problems in Venezeula obliged the makers to move their factory to the neighbouring Caribbean island of Trinidad.

The town also had an important place in the fight for independence from Spain. Bolívar came here to rebuild his shattered forces in 1817, and it was here that he received crucial reinforcements in the form of 5000 British veterans of the recently ended Napoleonic wars – his agents had recruited them in London. Two years later, in February 1819, the congress of Angostura proclaimed the formation of Gran Colombia; the building where its delegates met still stands on the central Plaza Bolívar.

Ciudad Guayana, a new city built since the early 1960s at the confluence of the Orinoco and Caroní rivers, is the centre of the economic development of the Orinoco lower region.

Venezuela's most beautiful city must be Mérida, set a mile high in wild Andean scenery and close to the Sierra Nevada National Park. Mérida is a university town founded in the 16th century, and is famous both for its lively carnival celebrations and the quality of the bullfights held here. It also has the Parque de las Cinco Repúblicas (Park of the Five Republics) with soil from the five republics Bolívar liberated: Venezuela,

Colombia, Panama, Ecuador and Peru. Indeed, the number five seems to have a special significance for Mérida, which is overlooked by the majestic snow-capped peaks known as the Five White Eagles. According to one local legend, these are all that remain of five Indian girls who were magically turned into mountains when they refused to surrender themselves to the invading *conquistadores*.

The Sierra Nevada, meanwhile, is a mountain paradise of tumbling streams and clear lakes. Venezuelans, tired of the pollution and pressures of the cities, come here to enjoy long hikes or horseback treks; trout fishermen explore the streams and lakes. Roads zigzag vertiginously up the mountainsides to towns and villages such as Bocanó, famous within Venezuela for its weavers and potters. Another small mountain town, Niquitao, celebrates Holy Week with special gusto. Large rolls of paper are distributed about the streets, so that the children can get together to produce a huge Easter mural.

At the same time, Venezuela is also a Caribbean country with tropical as well as mountain retreats. The island of Margarita – in fact, two islands linked by a long sandy spit – lies off the coast of Cumaná and offers all the usual pleasures of a Caribbean resort: golden beaches, expensive hotels and nightclubs, and glitzy shopping malls (taking advantage of the island's duty-free status), especially around the chief town Porlamar. But it has wilder parts, too: mangrove swamps, rich in shellfish; fertile wooded valleys in the interior of the eastern half; and scrubby dunes and marshes in the western Peninsula de Macanao, roamed by wild goats, hares and deer.

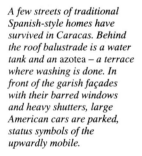

A few streets of traditional Spanish-style homes have survived in Caracas. Behind the roof balustrade is a water tank and an azotea *– a terrace where washing is done. In front of the garish façades with their barred windows and heavy shutters, large American cars are parked, status symbols of the upwardly mobile.*

Colombia

Wedged between the Andes and the Pacific and Caribbean seas,
Colombia boasts some of South America's most varied and
spectacular scenery – soaring mountain ranges, fertile river
valleys, windswept plains and swampy coastlands. It is a
supremely rich land: rich in beauty, rich in culture and rich in
valuable minerals. In recent decades, its infamous cocaine cartels
have grabbed world headlines, but Colombia has produced more
noteworthy lights than that, including its unofficial laureate, the
Nobel Prize winner and novelist Gabriel García Márquez.

Gold is still worked to pre-Columbian designs. In the Gold Museum in Bogotá, the legend of El Dorado *becomes a glittering reality, as visitors are transported back to the days of the* conquistadores.

Emeralds shine in the water of the river Muzo, like little fish. According to Chibcha legend, these gems are the tears of Fura, the first woman, who was punished for her adultery by the supreme god Are: Fura and her husband, Tera, were made mortal and Tera, in his despair, committed suicide. The gods were so moved by Fura's sorrow that they turned her tears into emeralds.

Previous page: In Villa de Leyva, villagers in their ruanas (ponchos) wait for a taxi. Little has changed here since colonial times.

Land of Coffee, Emeralds and Music

Christopher Columbus, the discoverer of the Americas, never visited the country which – after being known for three centuries of turbulent history as the New Kingdom of Granada – eventually bore his name. But later Spanish adventurers most certainly did. It was from Cartagena on the Spanish Main that the treasure galleons set sail, loaded with the Inca riches of neighbouring Peru. During the 16th century, they carried off three times as much bullion as existed in the whole of Europe – when the pirates would let them. Wealth of another kind now leaves Colombia nightly in rattling cargo planes, thanks to Colombia's dubious status as capital of the global cocaine cartels.

Between the seas

The only South American country with coasts on both the Pacific and the Caribbean, Colombia is the fourth largest republic in South America. It has an extraordinary and varied landscape: soaring mountains, dense jungles, fertile valleys and deltas, and extensive grasslands. The western two-fifths of the country lie in the highlands and valleys of the Andes mountains; while the rest, east of the Andes, consists of the *llanos* of the Orinoco Plains, the *selva* (rain forest) of the Amazon basin and a tiny strip of lowland along the Caribbean Sea.

The western highlands are sub-divided by four great, north-south mountain ranges. From west to east these are the Cordillera del Chocó, the Cordillera Occidental, the Cordillera Central and the Cordillera Oriental. The Western Cordillera has five peaks over 13,000 feet, but the Central Cordillera is higher, with six peaks over 16,000 feet. The Eastern Cordillera, the longest of the three, branches off into Venezuela, and its highest points are above 17,000 feet.

Colombia's three main rivers – the Atrato, Cauca and Magdalena – run northwards through the depressions between these mountain ranges into the Caribbean. It is in this area that Colombia's major cities, Bogotá and Medellín, are to be found; indeed, 98 per cent of the 33 million inhabitants live in the western two-fifths of the country. Here, too, are the plantations that produce Colombia's most famous export crop – its coffee. High-quality coffee has for long made up over a third of Colombia's cash-generating exports and sustained a rich agricultural heartland. Cali lies farther to the south in the Cauca Valley, Colombia's richest farmland.

The Pacific lowlands are sparsely populated, while on the Atlantic side, the bulk of the nation's commerce moves through the ports of Santa Marta and Cartagena. To the east, the lightly populated *llanos* constitute nearly 60 per cent of the country's total area and give way to unexplored tropical jungle in the south-east. Height above sea level, rather than distance from the Equator, is what determines Colombia's varied climate. The scalding Caribbean sun of Cartagena seems a world away from the often grey and chilly skies of the mountain capital, Bogotá.

The coastal *tierra caliente* (hot zone) extends to

Exploited first by the Indians and then by the Spanish, the mines at Muzo and Chivor were swallowed up by the jungle. Their whereabouts were unknown for several centuries, until they were rediscovered by a Colombian engineer using old Spanish documents.

Emeralds shine from blocks of grey stone. They have been torn from the Colombian earth at a cost of tons of dynamite, thousands of man-hours and quite probably a few lives. The gems will change hands several times, each time increasing in price, as they make their way to Bogotá.

about 3000 feet, with an average daytime temperature of 27°C (80°F) and some of the world's heaviest rainfall, favouring exuberant tropical flora and fauna. The *tierra templada* (or temperate zone) extends from 3000 feet to 6000 feet and supports slopes carpeted in forest, though much has been cleared for Colombia's coffee plantations, and for its infamous plantations of marijuana and coca (from which cocaine is refined). The *tierra fría* (cold zone) climbs for a further 6000 feet above the temperate zone: a cloud-enshrouded forest of low trees and shrubs, festooned with mosses and vines. Above that there is nothing but snow.

The hunt for gold

Since 1513, when the *conquistador* Vasco Nuñez de Balboa first sighted the Pacific Ocean from Colombian territory, the country has been cloaked in violence and intrigue. Simón Bolívar, who liberated South America from Spanish rule, perished here after his dream of creating a Greater Colombia (Gran Colombia) foundered. This century has scarcely been kinder to Colombia, which in the late 1950s emerged from *La Violencia* – an extraordinary 10-year outburst of mass political killings – just in time to be swept by a fresh wave of killings, this time inspired by drug traffickers. Bogotá is one of the world's more dangerous capitals, in which roving gangs care little if a stolen ring comes with a finger attached.

Despite its grim reputation, Colombia is a spectacular country whose people are relaxed, humorous and hospitable; its people have, after all, been receiving visitors for many centuries. Precious stones apart – and it produces 95 per cent of the world's emeralds – the country is rich in romance. More than 50,000 pre-Columbian gold artefacts on view in the Bogotá Museum of Gold recall ancient civilisations ruthlessly wiped out by the *conquistadores;* as do the large stone sculptures of San Agustín in the south-west of the country and the 'Lost City' of the Tayrona Indians near the Caribbean coast in the north.

The search for *El Dorado*, the mythical city of gold, drove the exploration of Colombia and indeed of South America. The quest began from Santa Marta, on the Caribbean, which was founded in 1525, and from Cartagena, farther south on the same coast, which was established eight years later. It was from these two settlements that the *conquistadores* made their way up the Magdalena river and into the great central Andean plateau and the heart of Colombia. Gonzalo Jiménez de Quesada and Sebastian de Belalcázar, a lieutenant who deserted the command of Peru's conqueror Francisco Pizarro, came here around 1530 to investigate Peruvian reports of the Chibchas.

According to reports, this tribe had 'so much gold that they offer it to Bachue, the mother of all men. . . . Each year, the *zipa* [tribal chief] pays tribute to Bachue. Accompanied by other men of high rank, he sails out to her in a boat full of gold and emeralds. His naked body is anointed with oil and covered with gold dust. The *zipa* throws himself into the waters of Lake Guatavita to offer the gold off his body to the goddess.'

The Chibchas, who lived on the Cundinamarca Plateau over 350 miles due south of the first Spanish settlement of Santa Marta, were finally found, but the little band of Spanish soldiers learned to their dismay that the custom of *El Dorado* had been abandoned centuries before. They were rewarded with considerable quantities of gold and precious stones, but nothing approaching the *El Dorado* of their dreams. Instead, these early colonists founded their new capital Santa Fé de Bogotá on the site of Bacatá, the centre of the displaced *zipa* culture. They found themselves rulers of a country which they named the New Kingdom of Granada.

The early days were hardly tranquil, however. Three groups – led by Jiménez de Quesada, by Belalcázar, and by a German named Nicolas de Federmann – often came to blows during the discovery and division of the country, and the Holy Roman Emperor Charles V had to step in to ensure peace. The new rulers eventually found themselves with an astonishingly varied colony which they would control for almost 300 years, until Bolívar ousted them in 1819 after the Battle of Boyacá.

Colombia is essentially a *mestizo* nation, its population a result of centuries of interbreeding between Europeans, Indians and, to a lesser extent, blacks. The

Opposite: *In Cartagena, the canopied façades of the houses contrast with the austere forts built by Philip II, king of Spain, to protect the port from pirates.*

Alongside its modern tower blocks, Colombia still has many buildings of the colonial 18th century such as these with their large round tiles, and barred and shuttered windows overlooking courtyards.

In the evenings on the Caribbean beaches of Colombia you can watch an evocative dance called cumbia, *the dance of love. The woman, bearing a lighted torch, weaves circles round her man, who feigns indifference before being finally caught up in the dance.*

vast majority of Colombians are of mixed blood; whites constitute an estimated 20 per cent of the population, blacks 4 per cent, and Indians 1 per cent. Historically, whites have occupied the higher social strata and have held most positions of power in the traditional elite which dominates national life. Coffee and other crops made Colombia something of an island of prosperity, if not of peace. But latterly the continuing violence, which in 1989 led to the murder by drug traffickers of the presidential candidate Luis Carlos Galán, has forced large numbers to seek their fortunes in Venezuela or *El Norte* (the United States).

Of Colombia's 33 million people, almost 400,000 are Indians (though half the nation has some Indian blood). Most of these people are concentrated in the highland regions, making up the Chibcha, Quimbaya and Agustinian tribes. In the Amazon forest regions close to Leticia, Indian peoples are hard at work producing handicrafts for the increasing numbers of visitors who come to see them. Equally striking – and a reminder of how close are Cuba and the other sugar-producing islands – is the community of pure black African descendants living on the Caribbean coast.

Though the twin heritage of Spain and the Roman Catholic Church is evident everywhere, the English language and Protestant faith maintain a toehold in San Andrés and Providencia – Colombia's Caribbean islands off the Nicaraguan coast, which once belonged to Britain. Colombians pride themselves on speaking the best Spanish on the continent, and boast that they even keep alive some courtly traditions from medieval Spain that have long been forgotten in the mother country. In the mountainous region of Santander, close to the frontier with Venezuela, it is said of the menfolk that 'they are aristocrats, heroes of the independence struggle, but modern life has not come close to them. They continue to dedicate themselves to the cults of honour and of courtly behaviour as in bygone days.' Verbal flourishes which became obsolete in Spain in the 18th century continue to be used in Colombia. No contrast could be greater than the one between these refined Colombians from the interior and their brash, wealthy Venezuelan neighbours.

Santander is named after Francisco de Paula Santander, the Colombian revolutionary who first aided Simón Bolívar and who, as a reward, was made vice-

The spindle used by this Colombian woman to spin her wool is used throughout the Andes. Here, however, she is using a primitive yet ingenious forked tripod to hold the bundle in place.

president of the newly independent Gran Colombia. Later, after clashing with the Liberator, he was suspended from office and eventually banished. However, after Gran Colombia was dissolved in 1830, he became president of the territories which today comprise Colombia and Panama.

Queen of the Indies

The coastal cities of those first *conquistadores* have survived and flourished. Cartagena de las Indias, founded in 1533 by Don Pedro de Heredia, is still surrounded by the massive walls that were built to protect its treasure-houses from pirates and rival navies throughout the 16th and 17th centuries. It was sacked by Sir Francis Drake, who shelled the cathedral, and by other freebooters, but by 1741 it was well-defended enough for a local hero, Don Blas, to repulse an attack by the British admiral Henry Vernon. The castle of San Felipe de Barajas, built in 1657, conceals a warren of underground tunnels in which the legendary gold was hidden.

In the 17th century Cartagena was, after Mexico City, the most important city in the New World. Although it declared independence from Spain in 1811, years of fighting followed. In 1815, during the battle for independence, Cartagena was captured by Spanish loyalists under Pablo Morillo and earned itself the nickname *La Heroica*. Nationalist forces prevailed in 1821, and Cartagena was incorporated into Colombia.

A city of 850,000 people, Cartagena is today a bustling trading centre. But in the old quarter, the streets are narrow and winding, and the buildings have finely wrought Spanish-style balconies sheltered beneath colourful canopies. It is a cheerful, noisy place, but it also contains some grim reminders of the brutality of Spanish colonialism and the slavery on which it was built. The Palace of the Inquisition, for instance, is a graceful example of baroque architecture. But it was here, from 1610 onwards, that the Church persecuted any leanings toward African animism along this Caribbean coast. The 17th-century La Popa monastery and the Gold Museum are reminders of how the twin terrors of God and Mammon shaped Colombia's history. The metals of Latin America were the means to finance the Inquisition's medieval crusade against modern forces both at home and in the colonies.

The Catholic faith in Colombia – the only recognised religion – has its dark side, with the Colombian people expressing a profound awareness of sin. At the Holy Week processions in the village of Monpox, participants wear gruesome masks in order to instil a fear of Hell. This interest in death and damnation is a legacy from Spain, but in Cartagena one is also aware of an equally powerful love of life. The country's most celebrated and exhilarating dance, the *cumbia*, was born here. The women, in long, flounced white dresses, carry lighted torches as they circle their partners who – also dressed in white, with crimson scarfs and straw hats – slash at the air with machetes. The choreography of the dance is explicitly sexual and symbolic: the torch-bearing women are dancing to re-kindle their men's ardour after their return, exhausted, from the fields.

Cockfights satisfy the Colombians' taste for violence and gambling. They are commonplace throughout the country and, in Cauca and Magdalena, the people hold special festivals, known as the 'festivals of the fine cock'.

Farther along the coast, in the modern industrial town of Barranquilla, people are more serious and sedate, except during the week before Lent when Barranquilla draws tourists to its colourful carnivals. The city is transformed into what the locals call *una ciudad loca* – a crazy town. Crowds fill the streets day and night, dressed in outlandish costumes and masks. There are parades and floats; people dance the *merecumbé* in the streets, and sing a song telling how the cayman came to Barranquilla.

Here in Barranquilla, in the bar La Cueva, Colombia's most famous son, the novelist Gabriel García Márquez, celebrated his first success as a writer. In Europe, García Márquez is considered a 'magic realist'; in Colombia he is known simply as a realist, for his *One Hundred Years of Solitude* is a story of everyday life in a tattered El Dorado called Macondo, a place much like García Márquez's native Aracataca. He was awarded the Nobel Prize for Literature in 1982. His portrayals of the barbarism, squalor and corruption of Latin American dictatorship consolidated his worldwide fame. By drawing on the popular culture of Colombia, and retelling the stories of travelling singers or raconteurs, Márquez has done much to rescue the country from oblivion and to convince intellectuals that such popular culture has massive power.

The ancient city of Santa Marta is the Caribbean coast's other gem. Though it was the first Spanish settlement, little remains from this era, apart from the Gold Museum which contains the stunning work of the Tayrona Indians. It was in Santa Marta that Simón Bolívar arrived penniless and sick in 1830, after his dream of a Gran Colombia (composed of what are now Venezuela, Colombia, Panama and Ecuador) had been shattered by the political machinations of his colleagues. He was given refuge at the plantation of the Marquis de Meir y Benitez, called San Pedro Alejandrino, three miles south-east of the city. Here Bolívar died of tuberculosis at the age of 47. Though his remains are in Caracas, some of his belongings have been gathered here.

Santa Marta, however, is no place for melancholic thoughts. Its *caribeño* population resolutely enjoys life, and the atmosphere here is infectious. Those with a taste for nightlife and for rum with coconut milk will relish this coast, lingering until the early hours of the morning under the palms, savouring *carimañolas* (fried cassava), rice with fish, rice with coconut, and the much-loved *arepas* (maize cakes).

In the mountains of the Sierra Nevada de Santa Marta lies that most romantic of prizes for any explorer, the Lost City. The Tayrona tribe of Caribbean Indians are a tall, gaunt, proud race who were described by the Spanish *conquistadores* as 'ferocious in battle, bloodthirsty, cannibalistic, sensual, worshippers of Buziraco, the spirit of evil'. For 400 years, they kept an astonishing secret: the location of the great city of their ancestors. In 1976 the site, which is considered to be the most important archaeological site in Latin America after Machu Picchu, was finally discovered by two pilots who happened to be flying over the mountains. The government stepped in to hinder a new generation of *conquistadores* – Colombian grave-robbers – from wrecking a sacred city that once supported a population of more than 3000 and was still partially inhabited by a handful of desperately poor Indian families.

Traces of the original city can be seen in the system of terracing and paved paths that survived even after its wooden buildings had been burned. It can be reached – expensively – by helicopter, or by a week-long trek

The morpho, *the 'great metallic blue', is an enormous butterfly common throughout the valleys and forests of Colombia.*

Peasants drying marijuana leaves in the Sierra de Perija. The big drug cartels are far better organised than this. They use aeroplanes to spray their vast plantations with fertilisers and insecticides.

Other peasants are employed in the cultivation of flowers; indeed, the savannah of Bogotá is known as the El Dorado of flowers.

through jungles, where visitors are advised to turn a blind eye to signs of marijuana plantations or left-wing guerrilla activity.

Farther up the coast from Santa Marta, towards the Venezuelan border, live another indigenous people, the Guajira Indians. Tall, slender and very beautiful, these barefoot nomads are renowned for their weaving. Unfortunately, in recent years, they have discovered that 'civilisation' puts a higher price on drugs than it does on crafts, and have become deeply involved in the trafficking of cocaine and marijuana. The ferocity with which they protect their illegal trade has made the region effectively a no-go area for outsiders.

Inland from Santa Marta, the Magdalena river valley is a wealthy region where bananas, cotton and rice grow in abundance. These crops are farmed by *criollos* of mixed Indian, white and black descent. They live in wooden houses, weave hammocks and straw hats, and produce beautiful naive paintings. Cultural highlights include the *corralejas* (bullfights), as well as yet another Colombian dance, the *vallenato* – a cocktail of sexuality and innocence. At Sincelejo, for example, the bullfights draw their inspiration from the festivals of San Fermín in the Basque country, where all the men are expected to run in front of the bull. Other demonstrations of *machismo* occur during the festivals of cockfighting.

Bogotá the urbane

Not far from the volcanic lake of the Laguna de Guatavita – into whose waters the Chibcha may once have plunged their gold-dusted *zipa* – lies the capital, Bogotá. Today the capital is home to more than 6 million people, almost 20 per cent of the country's population, but as recently as 1948 it was no more than a town. There is still an old colonial quarter named La Candelaria, with narrow, sloping streets, old lanterns and windows guarded by metal grilles; but today these streets run parallel to busy four-lane boulevards lined with glass-sheathed skyscrapers.

At the heart of the old city lies the Plaza de Bolívar, which is bounded by the Congress building, the rebuilt Palace of Justice, and the Cathedral. This beautifully situated city lies 8600 feet above sea level and its layout can best be seen from the hill of Monserrat, reached by cable-car. Founded in 1538, the capital is sometimes known as the 'Athens of America', because of the active intellectual life of its various universities. Colonial churches from the 17th and 18th centuries have survived better than other buildings in a city which, for all its urbanity, has done little to preserve its past.

In 1717 the city became the capital of the viceroyalty of New Granada, and a century later the capital of Bolívar's Gran Colombia. With the 1830 dissolution of the federation, Bogotá became the capital of a smaller republic of Colombia. The 19th century was dominated by a long battle between Liberals and Conservatives, which culminated in a bloody civil war from 1899 to 1903. There was more conflict during *La Violencia*, from 1948 to 1957, which resulted in an estimated 300,000 deaths: even a military coup failed to halt the strife.

The repression of peasant organisations by the army resulted in many more deaths. Though the guerrillas became involved with the drug traffickers, the latter have long outstripped them as a threat to the state. So arrogant have the cartels become that they even offered to pay off Colombia's national debt in exchange for freedom from arrest. Their only fear, it seems, is extradition to face trial in the United States.

Selling the contents of Bogotá's Gold Museum would also more than pay off Colombia's debts. The 50,000 stunning pieces of pre-Columbian gold on display – necklaces, diadems, nose rings and pectorals – mercifully escaped the Spanish habit of melting down

Opposite: A Tayrona woman guides her beast of burden along a mountain path. The Tayronas, whose 'Lost City' in the Sierra Nevada was discovered only recently, are a philosophical people concerned solely with matters of the spirit. Selected children are brought up and initiated into the mysteries of their ancient religion.

This small gourd contains a limestone powder which the Arhuacos ingest using a stick, along with a coca leaf to increase the hallucino-genic effect.

Spanish missionaries forced the Indians to renounce Buziraco, the Spirit of Evil, accusing these survivors of the 'Lost City' of lasciviousness and cannibalism. Modern anthropologists, however, are anxious to see their civilisation preserved.

the jewellery for tawdry crucifixes or coins. Upstairs is the breathtaking emerald display. But perhaps the most evocative piece in the whole collection is a gold statue of the unfortunate *zipa* in his magical boat.

After leaving the museum, you might be tempted by the array of gold and emerald jewellery displayed in the windows of the boutiques of the colonial quarter. But beware of showing off that newly acquired ring, for there are thieves in the street who are more than ready to tear it off your finger.

One of the saddest features of Bogotá are the bands of *gamines*, homeless children aged between six and ten, who have been reduced to roaming the streets, picking pockets and grabbing handbags. Some of them will grow into fully fledged violent criminals.

Violence is a fact of life in Bogotá, as it is in Medellín, Cali and the other major cities of Colombia. In 1948, the liberal leader, Jorge Eliécer Gaitán, was assassinated in Bogotá. His death provoked a popular uprising and 3000 people were killed in the repression which followed. The violence has not stopped since. Today it is perpetuated by guerrilla movements but above all by the drug traffickers. In the streets of Bogotá, adolescent boys follow tourists with the characteristic waddle of Hollywood bad-guys. Few of them know who their parents are, but all of them know about *yerba* (marijuana).

The true treasures of the region surrounding the capital are its flowers. Roses, carnations, tall, exotically blossomed strelitzias and many other species still grow wild along the waysides, and the rich agricultural land

Although Tunja lies at a height of some 10,000 feet, its market offers a wide variety of tropical fruits. The llanos *are not far away and contribute to the diversity of the produce.*

supports huge herds of dairy cows. This is a place of sudden contrasts: in a matter of minutes you move from the fresh spring air of the plain to the oppressive humidity of the port Girardot on the Magdalena river, where the only cool spot is the Guatavita Lagoon. The towns here still carry their Indian names – Fusagasuga and Facatativa, where the *zipas* built their strongholds, and where they, in turn, were tortured and killed by the *conquistadores* in pursuit of treasure.

To the east of Bogotá lies the Boyacá region, the sacred land of the Chibchas, where the finest emeralds in the world are mined. Tunja, the capital of the region, is a mixture of splendid colonial buildings (dating from its foundation in 1539) and peasant simplicity. If a single image characterises this region, it is that of a man in his white *ruanao* (poncho) passing cloisters, arches and white-washed houses with Spanish red-tiled roofs. It is Colombia's most fertile region, the vegetation as green as the stones for which it is famous. In the fields, men and women, black plaits hanging below their hats,

tend their crops of wheat. The region also supports vast herds of dairy cattle but the Indians have no stake in the wealth of these farms.

Farther north, in the region of Santander, the *cordillera* starts to break up. Tobacco, the main crop here, is processed in the huge cigar factories of Bucaramanga, capital of the region. Anyone who considers himself a fearless gourmand should watch out for the local culinary surprise, *hormiga culona* – fat-bottomed ant fried whole.

Big business in Medellín

Most Colombians are of mixed blood, but one of the exceptions to this are the *paisas* of Antioquia in the north-west Andes who are white. After their chiefs had committed suicide rather than surrender, the Indian population of this region died off in a series of wars with the Spanish. Nor were there ever any blacks in the

The Guambiano Indians still wear their traditional costume – blue skirts, crossed at the back.

Time has stood still at Villa de Leyva, a small town hidden in the folds of the Andes. This charming colonial house is not a museum, but a chemist's.

region either, since, apart from some quickly exhausted gold mines, there was nothing for slaves to do. The result of this accident is a Colombian with less taste for dancing *salsa* or drinking rum than for business – and a capital, Medellín, that is the second biggest industrial city in Colombia.

Founded in 1675, the capital of Antioquia was isolated until railways linked it to Bogotá. Government statistics claim that this is a coffee-growing region, and indeed it does produce a vast quantity of the product. But Medellín has become world renowned for a far less salubrious crop. The city is home to the nation's richest and most violent cocaine cartel. At the height of his power Pablo Escobar, its patriarch, possessed an impressive private zoo and financed entire housing projects for the poor. When eventually he gave himself up to justice, even his prison cell boasted five-star luxury – in any case, it was not long before he escaped.

Hugely wealthy, enormously powerful and totally ruthless, the drug barons effectively govern the region with their private armies. Despite the best efforts of Colombian politicians such as César Gaviria, Virgilio Barco and the full backing of the US Drug Enforcement Agency, anyone who stands in the way of the drug barons – police, politician or priest – is summarily killed. Nevertheless, Medellín has an amenable climate, splendid botanical gardens, smart shops and an elaborate infrastructure.

The extraordinary energies of these *paisas* have also been channelled in more positive directions for Colombia's benefit. Once the coffee plantations had declined in fertility, many of them spread out towards Colombia's remoter frontiers. Today the owner of a banana plantation in the Magdalena valley, or a trader in some out-of-the-way village on the Pacific coast, may turn out to be a *paisa*. Manuel Mejia Vallejo, the novelist, has described these pioneers setting off, machete in hand, to carve out a new future for themselves in the valleys of Caldas or Cauca. The people of Medellín, however, are not averse to pleasure. After Buenos Aires, this is the world's second home of the tango; and although Carlos Gardel, Argentina's most famous musician, died here in an accident, his memory lives on in the clubs and bars.

There are other more traditional forms of entertainment, including the *Desfile de Silleteros* (Flower Fair) in August, when the country people parade through the streets decked with flowers. If Gabriel García Márquez has immortalised the image of the lonely military dictator, then Colombia's bourgeoisie has been similarly captured by the country's other great contemporary artist, Fernando Botero, a native of Medellín. The fullness and depth of his subjects, and the irony with which he treats them, combine to make even children appear sinister.

Sugar and dance country

South of Medellín lies the Cauca valley and sugar country. Peasants with straw hats hack away with machetes at tens of thousands of acres of cane, just as they have done for centuries. The bus which runs between the two main towns, Cali and Popayán, is bright red and decorated with flowers. The Indians on

The best coffee bushes in the world grow in the red, volcanic soil of the Andes. Shaded by the leaves of the palm trees, the fruit ripens from green to red.

Each ripe coffee berry contains two seeds side by side which, when roasted, become coffee beans. There is a legend which tells how the Jesuits propagated coffee in Colombia: a priest who was partial to the drink used planting as a penance for his parishioners' sins.

board are Guambianos and wear a unisex costume which makes it difficult to differentiate between men and women: short black-and-pink-striped ponchos, black hats, red head-scarfs and short blue skirts.

Cali, the capital of the region, boasts the most beautiful women in the country, which is perhaps why it describes itself as *el paraíso de Colombia*. With their ebony-black hair and cinnamon skin, it is hardly surprising that these immensely elegant *caleñas* provided Latin America with its first romantic heroine, the love-lorn 'María' of Jorge Isaacs's novel – Isaacs was born in Cali of a wealthy English-Jewish father and published *María* (still one of Latin America's most famous novels) in 1867. Cali is also known as the capital of Colombian *salsa,* the dance that originated in Cuba.

Every June, Cali holds a national art festival when the city is alive with theatrical groups, and artists and sculptors exhibiting their works. It is also a good occasion to taste some of Colombia's extraordinarily rich traditions of music and dance. Dance groups perform the *bambuco,* the national dance, whose gently rhythmic strains – according to one story – gave renewed courage to the Colombian troops fighting at Ayacucho in 1824, the battle that liberated their Peuvian neighbours from Spanish rule. A small band sets the pace, with a *chuco* shaker establishing the rhythm, and a flute and small, 12-stringed guitars – known as *tiples* – providing the melody. The dancers, meanwhile, execute a series of complex steps and figures, each with a special name suggestive of the drama being acted out:

the Invitation, the Flirtation, the Pursued. The female dancer is finally left on her knees.

The *bambuco* is essentially a dance of Colombia's highland regions – the other regions too have their special traditions. African influence is strongest along the Pacific coast, where dances such as the *marimba* predominate, with various kinds of drums setting a mesmerising percussive rhythm. The Caribbean coast is home to Colombian *salsa* with a more swinging Latin pace. The *llanos* of the east specialise in dances for couples such as the galloping *corrido* and sinuous, heel-tapping *joropo.*

After Carli, the Pan-American Highway continues to Popayán, one of Colombia's most beautiful colonial cities, which was founded in 1537. Though an earthquake destroyed some old buildings in 1983, many of the whitewashed colonial mansions have survived, and the city's charm with it. During Easter Week, Popayán is home to some of the country's most notable religious processions.

North-east of here is the Tierradentro district, an extraordinary archaeological zone of underground burial chambers or circular tombs from the pre-Columbian era. From the town of San Andrés de Pisimbalá, you can hire horses to visit the four sites, the most important of which is Segovia. There are more than 20 tombs here, carved out of the soft rock; they once contained ceramic funerary urns, and are decorated with geometric patterns and drawings.

Southwards on the highway lies Pasto. Where the *caleños* are cheerful, vivacious and sensual, the *pastusos* are slow, calm and methodical. This is a town of almost a dozen churches, the most notable of which is the Cristo Rey close to the central square, which has fine stained-glass windows. The people are great wood-carvers – a craft which has been handed down from generation to generation since pre-Columbian times (the

The coffee berry is picked by hand, opened and the twin seeds removed. They are left to steep in vats, then washed and dried in the sun: the end product is the famously smooth Colombian coffee.

The fruit of the cacao tree is large and hard, and contains up to 40 strongly flavoured cacao nibs. These are held in a soft pulp which gradually dries out as the fruit ripens.

ancestors of the Indians of this region, the Quellasingas, formed part of the Inca empire). Their speciality is a decorated varnish technique called *barniz de Pasto*. Three-quarters of the local population are involved in wood-carving and other crafts, such as leatherwork, weaving, ceramics and jewellery.

East of Pasto, the character of the people changes. Those who inhabit the banks of the Magdalena river are as excitable as the Colombians of the Caribbean. It is an eerie region, however, once prosperous but now largely abandoned – a graveyard of roofless churches, unused bridges and ghost towns scattered along the riverside. But towns have survived and, in some cases, even prospered: in Barrancabermeja it is because of oil; in Girardot, tourists from Bogotá; in Tolima, rice and cotton.

Neiva, the capital of the Huila region, is the place from which to approach San Agustín, the biggest attraction in south-west Colombia and one of the most important archaeological sites in the Americas. There are any number of theories to explain the mysterious

At a cattle market in the llanos *region, cattle outnumber people by fourteen to one.*

civilisation which left behind hundreds of free-standing stone statues, rather similar to the mysterious giants of Easter Island. There are underground tombs, too, but it is the statues, some 500 of which have been excavated, that are most powerful. These fantastic stones – the largest of which is almost 13 feet high – appear to depict forest animals as well as mythical monsters. Jaguars, frogs, eagles clawing and grasping their prey, lizards and cats, all are there to guard the entrance to the burial chambers.

Just who the Agustinians were is an enigma: like so many other Andean civilisations, they probably succumbed to the expanding Inca empire, though this would have marked the extreme northern limit of Inca territories. The culture, of which this was some kind of ceremonial centre or burial place, probably flourished

between the 6th century BC and 13th century AD. One theory is that these statues are the work of Mayans who had emigrated south from homelands in Central America. It is known, however, that during the period of occupation there were two complete changes of population. San Agustín is an amazing place, set in the rolling green landscape of coffee plantations and riven by deep gorges and waterfalls.

The sculptures are scattered across what must once have been sacred ground in a canyon formed by the Magdalena river. The Archaeological Park near the town contains about 150 sculptures, as well as tombs and burial mounds spread through the Bosque de las Estatuas. The other site, Alto de los Idolos, has some massive stone sarcophagi and the largest of the statues in the region.

The best way to explore the statues is on horseback, when suddenly and unexpectedly, these life-sized stone monsters with their terrifying gestures rear up in front of the visitor.

Jungle fortunes

The jungles of Colombia's Pacific coast lie in the world's most rain-drenched region. It is here that the Pan-American Highway, that grand scheme to link the Americas, quite literally got bogged down.

Fabulously rich in gold and platinum, the region swarms with fortune hunters, desperately seeking riches at the bottom of disused mine shafts and insect-infested swamps. There are few tourists to this part of Colombia,

The llaneros *are the traditional cattlemen of the Colombian plains. They are proud, independent people who were recruited by Simón Bolívar in his struggle against Spanish colonialism.*

This child's necklace is both ornamental and talismanic. Since the Spanish conquest, Indians have used their magic against the white man, unfortunately with little advantage to themselves.

for it is an inhospitable place, its customs as impenetrable as the jungle itself. The main town of the Chocó region, Quibdó, is really accessible only by aeroplane, and beyond that, the only route through the jungle is by boat along the Atrato river. Though the Cauca Valley Authority is trying to ensure that development is orderly, the environmental destruction brought about by new roads leading to cattle ranches and clandestine coca plantations bodes ill for the forest's survival.

The awful poverty of the mainly black population in this region stands as a great contrast to the myth of *El Dorado,* or the sudden riches that may be plucked from a riverbed in the form of an emerald. The crafts of the region, however, are superb and include gold work, with a particular emphasis on filigree. There is also a rich musical tradition. Here African rhythms blend with native Indian tunes and 16th-century Spanish ballads. Thanks to the isolation of this region, these tunes, known as *currulao* and *bunde*, have survived unchanged over the centuries. Little changed, too, are the traditions of the Chocó Indians, groups of whom dwell in thatched-roofed huts on the riverbanks and have only recently substituted their blowpipes for modern firearms.

Just off the Pacific coast are a string of islands with

Indians of north Santander soak banana leaves in the river water. Once they are supple, these leaves are used in a variety of ways, from roofing houses to wrapping and preserving food.

beguiling names such as La Viciosa (woman with many vices), or Gorgonilla (the little Gorgon). But the islands for which Colombia is most famous lie in the Caribbean off Nicaragua's Mosquito coast: San Andrés and Providencia. Perhaps because these islands lay close to the shipping lanes along which the treasure-laden galleons headed for Spain, they changed hands frequently. But the British finally prevailed – until the period of independence when Colombia seized the islands. Colonial-style clapperboard houses and an easy-going, English-speaking population are a legacy from the days of British rule.

Today San Andrés offers Colombians a tax-free shopping paradise, but most visitors come here for the extraordinary underwater life of the coral reefs. Nearby Providencia looks a perfect place in which to hunt for pirate treasure. And so it should be: Captain Henry Morgan, the Welsh buccaneer, is reputed to have left his hoard here, rather than at Cueva de Morgan, the underwater cave on San Andrés.

Until 1903 Colombia included modern Panama. But with the help of the United States (which provided warships in exchange for the rights to dig a canal), this province broke away. Today only the Darién Gap – a still-forbidding 80-mile strip of jungle and swamp that was once a bottleneck impeding travel between two continents – remains of Colombia's former territory.

Home of the cowboys

Three-fifths of Colombia's territory lies to the east of the Andes, yet only about 2 per cent of the population lives there. This vast tract of land – more than a quarter of a million square miles – divides into two distinct regions, the *llanos* (plains) in the north, and the Amazon jungle in the south. The *llanos* are the continuation of the vast plains of Venezuela. The plains are good hunting country, and abound in jaguar, wild boar, alligator, deer, puma and tapir. Dry, hot and forbidding, they are also home to the *llaneros*, or itinerant cowboys. Ask one how he sees the world and he may say: 'I'm on the top of my horse and above me there's only my hat.'

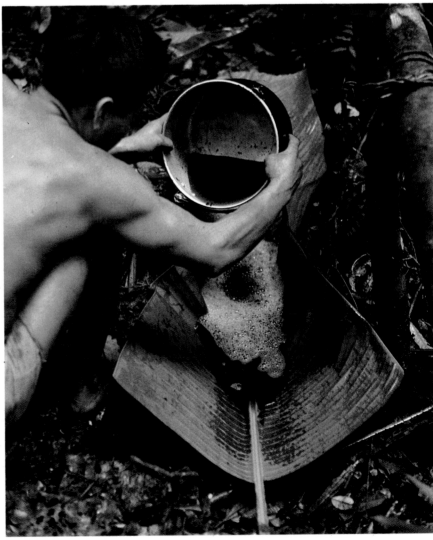

This Amazon Indian is carrying an armadillo, an armour-plated animal with nine bands of hard, over-lapping scales. The armadillo is nocturnal and difficult to hunt, but it is much sought after as a delicacy.

An Amazon Indian mixes curare in a banana-leaf trough. Death from curare, a deadly poison which paralyses the respiratory system and is used on arrow tips, occurs within seconds.

These men are comparable with the Argentinian *gaucho*. The *llaneros* are fiercely independent and melancholic; indeed, it was these horsemen who were recruited by Simón Bolívar in his fight for Latin American independence. If history has passed them by since then, the region is making up for lost time with a flurry of oil exploration. It is believed that huge reserves lie beneath the scrubland. The capital, Villavicencio, is in the far west of the region at the foot of the Andes. It is cooled in the evening by breezes from the nearby mountains, but in the daytime, temperatures rise well over 32°C (90°F). Villavicencio is a cattle town with one claim to fame: it is the source of the Orinoco river, itself the life-force of the *llanos*.

Colombia's 'empty quarter' is its eastern Amazon province. The chronicler Juan de Castellanos, writing at the time of the Spanish conquest, put it quite simply: 'The trees are enormous and mad'. He went on to describe virile Indian women, and – according to one of many theories on the subject – their courage may have inspired Captain Francisco Orellana to name the river 'Amazon'. Standing in the basin of the river, it is easy to see how Castellanos's imagination ran riot. Latterly, the writer José Eustasio Rivera has described eloquently the horrors of the Amazon region: of the invasions of ants which devastate an entire village in a few minutes; of trees that drip poison; and of the *Victoria regia*, a giant lotus flower which can bear the weight of a child, but which can also serve as a hiding-place for deadly piranha fish.

A dogleg of territory cutting southward from the Putumayo allows Colombia access to the Amazon river itself, and it is here that the country's farthest outpost is situated. Leticia is the only town of any size on the Colombian Amazon, sitting right on the border with both Brazil and Peru. Leticia's main function is that of a gateway to Brazil and the lower Amazon: its climate is unbearable and its insects voracious.

For those going no farther than Leticia, a boat trip up the river itself allows the visitor to see manatees (aquatic mammals native to the Amazon) as well as scores of bird species unique to the region. There are 120 different types of hummingbird alone; then, of course, there are parrots and thousands of monkeys. The best place to see wildlife close to the town is the Monkey Island, where thousands of small yellow-foot monkeys come to stare at passing boats. Local travel agents arrange trips up the Atacuari river. A visit to the Parque Nacional Amacayacu allows a better insight into the rain forest ecosystem and its peoples. Visitors can stay with the Yagua people – who, together with the Ticunas, form the main Indian nation here – and study their customs. Several indigenous Indian peoples – the Cuibas, Mellao, Chiricoas, Yomu, Tunebos, Yagua and Piapocos – still live as they have done for centuries, supporting themselves by hunting and fishing.

The Putumayo river, which forms the border between Peru and Colombia, is peaceful now. But less than a century ago it was lawless, unclaimed territory. It was here that Julio César Araña enslaved Indians in their thousands. He was a Peruvian using British capital to consolidate an immense rubber trading business over an area of jungle the size of Belgium. He treated those who refused to gather rubber for him with unspeakable cruelty, and by 1910 half the Indians in the region had perished, many simply to ensure his wealth.

The Amazon jungle is home to a range of different, but all equally noisy, species of parrot, including the green, the yellow and blue Ara ararauna, *and the macaw. At around 7pm, however, as the sun sets, they all fall silent.*

At the end of the day, men, women and children retire to their hammocks. Around them dogs, hens and bristly black pigs seek comfort from the hard earth.

Bolivia

Myth and tradition cling fast to a mountainous land, much of it
cradled between two great ranges of the Andes. Bolivia's Quechua
and Aymara peoples account for more than half its population,
and keep alive a rich pageantry of festivals and customs that long
predate the Spanish Conquest. The country is also home to the
fabled 'mountain of silver' Potosí, source of much of the fabulous
wealth of the former Spanish Main. More recently, it has acquired
a different reputation, for political instability – with nearly 200
governments in less than 170 years of existence.

Previous page: *La Paz is one vast, colourful but silent market; these tradeswomen, or* cholas, *never cry their wares.*

Right and below: *Llamas and vicuñas graze the small, grass-covered mounds of the high plains.*

Mountain Bastions of an Ancient World

Landlocked Bolivia, today the poorest country in South America and the only one in which Indians outnumber those of European descent, is often likened to Tibet. Indeed, the strange ability of its people to eke out a living in the high lunar-landscaped plateau of the Altiplano, overlooked by snow-capped peaks, enhances the feeling of remoteness from the known world. Its mystery is increased by legends both old and new: of the ancient ruins associated with the Aymara-speaking peoples who established an empire here long before the Incas; and of Potosí, the mountain of silver that sustained the Spanish empire.

It was in Bolivia, too, that latterday heroes as various as Che Guevara and Butch Cassidy and the Sundance Kid all met violent deaths. Violence and instability have been endemic to Bolivia, which holds the mixed honour of having witnessed the largest number of coups d'état in history. It has had an unfortunate record in wars too: three times this century it has lost territory to its neighbours. But there is nowhere else on the continent where visitors can find such vibrant and colourful indigenous life.

Roof of a continent

Bolivia is the windswept roof of the South American continent. The Altiplano is one of the highest populated areas in the world, with an average elevation of about 12,000 feet, its surrounding peaks reaching up to three miles high. This is a chill, 80-mile-wide plateau of treeless desert where the circling condor or the llama may be the only living thing. The Altiplano is a land of superlatives: Lake Titicaca, the highest navigable lake in the world; La Paz is the highest capital, with the highest airport and the highest golf course. But the country also has fertile valleys (*yungas*), the vast featureless grasslands of the *gran chaco* which stretch away south-west towards Paraguay, and a generous swathe of sweltering, insect-ridden Amazon rain forest bordering on Brazil. Although considered an Andean nation, in fact almost two-thirds of Bolivian territory lies in the tropical lowlands.

The continent's fifth largest country is dominated by the Andes, which spread to their widest extent in Bolivia and are divided into two great *cordilleras*, separated by the Altiplano. The western *cordillera* forms Bolivia's border with Chile; its peaks rise to 23,012 feet at Nevada de Ancohuma, Bolivia's highest point. The eastern mountain chain is dominated by Illampu (21,231 feet) and Illimani (22,578 feet), and slopes toward the lowlands of the Amazon basin. Southwards from Cochabamba, the *cordillera* slopes toward the *gran chaco*. On the eastern face, steep-sided *yungas* cut deeply into the slopes, providing a niche for human habitation.

The Altiplano is simply too high for tree growth and has only the thinnest of vegetation. Yet the Beni plain to the north-east has extensive subtropical and tropical forests. Bolivia's animal life ranges from predators of the rain forest, such as the jaguar and anaconda snake, to the ostrich-like rhea, puma and deer in the *chaco* grasslands; while the highlands are inhabited by the llama and its relatives the alpaca, and vicuña and the grey squirrel-like chinchilla.

The Indian heritage

The population of Bolivia is just 7.3 million. Most Bolivians live in the arid, inhospitable uplands. In contrast to neighbouring Brazil, people of mixed race make up only one-third of the population, with a handful of descendants of African slaves brought to mine silver in the 16th century. Well over half the population is of pure Indian stock, still speaking one of two Indian languages, Quechua or Aymara, and as a

This plant, with its small yellow flowers, is almost as important to the Bolivian Indians as the food they eat. Coca grows wild in the Andes and has been cultivated on the mountain terraces for centuries. The Indians chew balls of coca leaves all day, which helps them cope with hunger, exhaustion and appalling living conditions.

result keeping alive a strong traditional culture.

Silent and inscrutable, Bolivia's Indians and their history are particularly intriguing to visitors. No one knows for certain, but it seems that in about 1500 BC the Aymara began settling the Altiplano. Several hundred years later, the Tiahuanaco culture coalesced around Lake Titicaca in the north. This technically advanced civilisation preceded the Incas by over 600 years, reaching its peak around AD 600. Though its influence may have stretched far beyond modern Bolivia's borders, it succumbed to the Quechua-speaking Incas.

The Aymaras of the high plains belonged for a time to Tahuantinsuyo – the Inca empire. The Incas themselves were Quechua Indians whose descendants still survive in the Bolivian valleys of Cochabamba and Sucre. The Incas' hold on this territory lasted just three centuries, before the Spanish in turn defeated them.

Though the Aymaras of the Altiplano can boast a civilisation whose beginnings substantially pre-date the Incas, little remains of their former greatness. For these people, with their ponchos, bowler hats, *ojotas* and multi-coloured woollen *chullos*, little has changed for the better – and much has been for the worse – with the passing of the centuries.

The Aymara Indians are a squat people with high cheekbones, slanting eyes and smooth bronze skin, looking rather like the Tibetans. They are truly a product of their environment: possessed of huge lungs that are needed to breathe the thin air at 12,000 feet above sea level; and with hearts of a size that never ceases to amaze European doctors. Without their incredible constitution, these people could never survive on this permanently wintery plain, where the average temperature is 5°C (40°F) and the changing seasons are marked only by periods of rain and drought.

The Altiplano produces limited supplies of tiny, hard, violet-coloured potatoes, beans, barley and an even smaller harvest of a grit-hard grain called *quinoa*. The Aymaras' only companions are the alpaca, vicuña and chinchilla, which provide wool, and the llama which is used as a beast of burden in a culture that has been resistant to the wheel. A few sheep, goats and scrawny cows are kept for meat which is generally dried in the sun to become *charqui*. That is the total range of their diet. The birds which soar overhead – ibis, gulls and condors – are part of the majestic landscape, but offer nothing in the way of nourishment.

The Quechua, descendants of the Incas who occupied the region from the 11th to the 15th centuries, betray this heritage in the pre-Columbian style of their stone houses, panpipe music, and in a mythology that is rooted in the past. Their villages are organised around kinship groups, and marriage partners are chosen from within the village. Until a generation ago most of these farmers used primitive techniques to grow potatoes and maize, usually as sharecroppers when they were not working as labourers on the big plantations. Now an

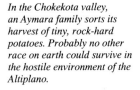

In the Chokekota valley, an Aymara family sorts its harvest of tiny, rock-hard potatoes. Probably no other race on earth could survive in the hostile environment of the Altiplano.

official language, Quechua is spoken by about 11 million Indians.

The Indians' survival on the Altiplano is due in no small part to coca. From morning to night they chew on balls of coca leaves (*acullico*) with the result that their lips and teeth are permanently stained green. The coca takes away hunger, coldness and fatigue and, with only an *acullico* for sustenance, they can cover incredible distances on foot in a single day. While the Aymaras are sedentary by nature, their environment is such that they are obliged to be constantly on the move, seeking better pastures for their flocks and more profitable markets for their produce.

Despite centuries of oppression by foreign masters, the Indians of the Altiplano have held on to many of their ancient traditions and beliefs. They are Christian but their religion exists in consort with a variety of animist cults. Life and spirit are attributed to everything, and everything is therefore divine. The Sun is *Inti*, incarnated in the immortal figure of the Inca; and the Moon is *Pajsi*, who marks the cycle of the agrarian year. The stars are *Warawara*; the wind *Hairarata;* the husband of Mother Earth, *Pachamama,* to whom the Aymaras offer the first taste of their *chicha,* an alcoholic maize drink; and the Rainbow is *Cumri* whose colours are said to be responsible for causing pregnancy in unmarried girls. The Devil is *Supay*, the governor of *socovón* – the mine shaft – and it is he who decides whether you return from the depths safely or are lost in darkness for ever. But the Aymara Devil is also the Satan of Christianity; for although the Indians have rejected the Spanish language, they continue to follow the religion of the *conquistadores*. It is as if they feel that the more divinities they have, the more protection they will receive.

Animals are also sacred to the Aymaras. The spirit of *Huasa Malluca* is incarnated in the puma; and the condor and vicuña are treated as totems. Sorcerers use lizards to heal, moths to kill, and armadillos to exact revenge on their enemies. Indians' necks are strung with amulets which promise the wearer love, fertility and protection against evil spirits. All these rituals exist, like some ancient, shadowy ancestor, alongside a flourishing Catholic church. The church has accepted the practice of syncretism, whereby pagan beliefs are observed openly. Thus, llama foetuses may be offered to the gods at celebrations held in cemeteries where adobe tombs are surmounted by Christian crosses. All Saints' Day merges with the cult of the *chulpas*, the tombs of the dead, and most Catholic ceremonies are accompanied by a pagan *challa*.

Stooped under the load in her striped aguayo, *this Indian woman spins wool as she walks.*

Every street corner becomes an open-air restaurant. The food is substantial: maize, quinza *(small grain rice), a little mutton and a great deal of chilli pepper.*

The adobe and thatch houses of the Altiplano blend with the landscape. The family cooks and eats outside, weather permitting, and sleeps in a single room on blankets of their own making; their weaving is one of the few bright things in an otherwise grey world.

A *challa* is an excuse to celebrate, and the Indians of the Altiplano love celebrations. Any number of events and anniversaries serve as a pretext to throw handfuls of confetti, which catch in the women's plaits and bowler hats. It could be a child's second birthday, or his first haircut (*ruthuchiku*) a baptism will do equally well, or indeed a marriage or house-warming. Celebrating is a serious business. It is not uncommon for an Aymara Indian to spend a year's wages on a carnival costume. There are carnivals to mark the Christian festivals of Christmas, Corpus Christi, the festival of the Cross and of John the Baptist, together with numerous traditional celebrations, notably the pilgrimage to the Copacabana sanctuary and the Carnival at Oruro.

The Spaniards captured the Great Inca in 1532 and, five years later, held Cuzco, the Peruvian capital from which the Incas' Bolivian territory (later called Alto Perú) was then being administered. The effect was immediate, as the *conquistadores* came in search of the legendary silver deposits. In 1538 Pedro de Anzures established the township of La Plata as the Spanish administrative centre; centuries later this blossomed into

Sucre. The hunt for wealth, inspired by Gonzalo Pizarro – younger half-brother of the Incas' conqueror, Francisco Pizarro – continued until 1545, when searchers stumbled upon a solid mountain of silver at Potosí. Millions of tons of the metal were extracted during the 16th and 17th centuries – and millions of slaves, both Indian and African, died to enrich the Spanish empire. In its heyday Potosí was a larger, richer and more advanced city than many in Europe.

For the Indians of both the Aymara and Quechua peoples, the Spanish conquest led to slavery. The *conquistadores* adapted the Inca system of serfdom (*mita*) and imposed a previously unknown degree of cruelty. The result was that, from 1530 to 1952, most Bolivian Indians lived in conditions of slavery, obliged to undertake unpaid work (*pongaje*) for their white masters. The many coups d'état and changes of government which have punctuated Bolivian history have had little effect on the lives of the Indians. It was only in 1952, when the Revolutionary Nationalist Movement took power, that they achieved a voice in government. Mines, previously in the hands of three mega-rich potentates – the families of Patiño, Hoschild and Aramayo – were nationalised, and sweeping agrarian reforms were introduced. Indians were freed from *pongaje* and were awarded tracts of land (*sayanas*). These changes did little to lessen the hardship and poverty of everyday life but they did at least give the Indians a degree of autonomy and self-respect.

Before the Indians could win their freedom, though, Bolivia had to liberate itself from the Spanish yoke. The first revolutionary rumblings came in 1781, when a half-hearted attempt was made to expel the Spanish and restore the Inca empire. But a more serious threat to Spanish power developed in Chuquisaca in 1809, when a provisional government was established and its revolutionary ideas began filtering through the continent. Bolivia – the only South American country named after a rebel against European colonisation – only declared its independence in 1824 after the Liberator Simón Bolívar had won battles at Junín and Ayacucho. Bolívar, the Venezuelan-born revolutionary,

was supported by General Antonio José de Sucre, who in 1826 became Bolivia's first president after defeating strong royalist resistance.

Ill-fated wars

Bolivia's troubles hardly ended there – in fact, in its first 164 years of existence it witnessed no fewer than 189 governments. At one stage, as a result of a confederacy with neighbouring Peru that displeased the Chileans, Bolivia had three governments in power at the same time. For a nation already cursed by conquest and chronic political instability, Bolivia has also been cursed by ill-luck in war. It has been roundly beaten by three of its five neighbours and has been forced to yield what could have been some of its most useful territories to them.

In the mid-19th century, the discovery of nitrate deposits in the Atacama Desert coastal region brought sudden wealth – though mostly to the Chilean merchants who were exploiting these minerals while under contract to the Bolivian government. Antofagasta was founded in 1866 to supply these nitrate mines and most of Bolivia's trade, primarily tin, went out through its only Pacific Ocean port. When Bolivia's government tried to tax these minerals, Chile's army seized the 175-mile coastline, cutting Bolivia off from the sea. The 1879-83 War of the Pacific was a disaster for Bolivia, which still claims a corridor to the coast.

The next piece of Bolivian territory to be broken off was the remote but rubber-rich Amazon territory of Acre, which was seized in 1903 by Brazil. Just as Chile tried to compensate Bolivia by offering it port facilities, so Brazil offered it access to the Atlantic, and helped to finance the Madeira-Mamoré railway which would have allowed it to reach the upper Amazon river – though it was never finished, and finally closed in 1972.

After disasters to the north and west, Bolivia's next misfortune was to the south. Skirmishing between Bolivia and Paraguay began in 1928 after the two sides had begun fortifying their borders; Bolivia had also demanded a new outlet to the sea through the Rio de la

A strong rush, called totora, *grows along the banks of Lake Titicaca* (right). *The Indians use it to build boats called* balsas (above), *which are strong and light. It is said that an Inca city built of solid gold lies at the bottom of the lake. Whatever the truth of this, the lake is rich in vegetation.*

Harvest time on the shores of Lake Titicaca. Indians have grown crops here since pre-Inca times.

Indian women pound maize. The cereal is a staple of indigenous populations throughout Latin America; it is to the Indian what rice is to the Asian.

Plata system, in order to compensate for the loss of the Atacama. The Chaco War, which raged between 1932 and 1935, was really a struggle over some featureless plains that had aroused little real interest until American geologists predicted, mistakenly, that oil lay underneath. The Indians suffered most from the war, with troops from the cold but disease-free Altiplano perishing like flies in the tropical heat.

It is not just the neighbours who have been upset by Bolivia, for the country even managed to infuriate Britain's Queen Victoria. In 1884, a diplomatic crisis developed in La Paz over a glass of *chicha* liquor. The newly appointed British ambassador to Bolivia was judged guilty of gross discourtesy when he sneered at the local brew served to him by the country's then dictator Mariano Melgarejo. As a penance for his rudeness, the hapless diplomat was forced to drink a barrelful of chocolate before being paraded through the streets sitting backwards on a donkey. News of the event so enraged Queen Victoria when she heard it that she demanded a map of South America and drew a cross through the offending nation. 'Bolivia,' she announced, 'does not exist!'

The Chaco War brought to the boil a potent mix of domestic conflict. In 1951 Víctor Paz Estenssoro, the leader of the National Revolutionary Movement which won the elections, was prevented from taking power by a rightist military coup. After the April Revolution, however, he embarked on 12 years of astonishingly progressive government that profoundly changed Bolivia. His numerous and far-reaching social reforms included nationalising the tin-mines, introducing universal suffrage, land reforms, and curbing the military. Paz Estenssoro was overthrown in a military coup in 1964, unleashing a dizzying alternation of coups and elections until the present day.

Some romance still clings to these struggles: in 1967 Ernesto 'Che' Guevara, the incendiary Latin American guerrilla leader who planned to spread the principles of Fidel Castro's Cuban revolution through the continent, breathed his last in Bolivia. After fruitlessly trying to train a Bolivian guerrilla force, he was captured and summarily executed by the army.

Thanks in part to these political disturbances, Bolivia still merits the description given by a French traveller a century ago of a 'beggar seated on a golden throne'. Bolivia has minerals aplenty – tin, copper, silver and gold – but the inaccessibility of many mines, together with their erratic management and the volatility of world prices, has played havoc with the economy. The

Coca has become a focus of superstition in Bolivia. Here at Copacabana, on the shores of Lake Titicaca, a young sorcerer is reading the future in sacred coca leaves cast on the ground.

At the witchcraft market you can buy dyes, medicinal herbs and magic potions. Whatever the problem – love, money or fertility – the answer lies in one of these colourful packets.

Most Bolivian cholas are traders. This woman will travel huge distances, carrying her aguayo, to take her produce to market.

The totora *reed of Lake Titicaca fulfils many functions. Here, a* chola *in La Paz is weaving the reed into crosses which she will sell in the street-markets.*

The Indians have their own doctors, the callahuaya. *These half-healers, half-sorcerers use herbs and hallucinogens. The* amantas (*wise men*) *claim to hear the mountains speak when they are under the influence of these potions.*

1985 crash in tin prices sent tens of thousands of starving miners to the slums of La Paz.

Thousands more poor miners turned to Bolivia's other economic lifeline – the cultivation of coca. In 1990 President Jaime Paz Zamora claimed that trade in the raw material from Colombia's cocaine laboratories accounted for almost three-quarters of Bolivia's income and half its exports. Bolivians have long been familiar with coca. Engravings from Inca times show that coca played an important part in pre-Columbian society. After the Conquest, Indians turned to the leaf to sustain them through centuries of slavery and hunger. The Spanish, of course, were well aware that plentiful supplies of coca increased the productivity of their

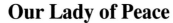

slaves with negligible expense on food. Plantations were established to help the silver-miners of Potosí beat cold and hunger. Today, the successors of those plantations still keep the country going.

Our Lady of Peace

The Altiplano is the country's industrial hub and home to the vast majority of its inhabitants. Nowhere else in the world does such an industrial region – with cities, highways and railways – flourish at such an altitude. Bolivia's capital city, La Paz rests in a natural basin at an altitude of over 10,000 feet, surrounded by towering, snow-capped mountains, and is the world's highest city.

La Paz was founded by the Spaniard Alonso de Mendoza in 1548, on the site of an Aymara village, after the discovery of gold in the Choqueyapu valley. Of greater importance than the gold was its role as a staging post for the mules bringing silver to the coast from Potosí, and it is now home to more than a million

people. The town was first named Nuestra Señora de La Paz (Our Lady of Peace) to commemorate the peaceful conditions then existing in Bolivia. The building of the railways further increased its importance. Despite its majestic setting, La Paz at first appears an ugly blur of orange brick and grey corrugated iron. A closer inspection reveals it to be one of South America's most unusual and colourful cities.

Three styles of architecture exist side by side: the luxurious but austere style of the Spanish colonial buildings around Alonso de Mendoza Square; the baroque 19th-century colonial style; and the modern, shabby skyscrapers of the commercial district. It is not the architecture, however, but the street life which makes La Paz such an enticing place to visit. Narrow alleyways stretch up the hillsides, crammed with Bolivian women in bright, layered dresses and bowler hats, selling blankets, nuts, herbs and – for the *gringos* (foreigners) – knitted jumpers with llamas on them. Here you will also find the *mercado de hechiceria* (the witchcraft market) where elderly Indian women sell charms for every eventuality: bottles containing

This christening in La Paz is a mixture of Christianity – illustrated here in the figure of Christ on the Cross – and pagan ritual. No celebration in Bolivia is complete without showers of multi-coloured confetti.

The icon of St Peter is carried in a procession by an Aymara woman. Catholicism plays an important part in the daily lives of Bolivian Indians. It has never, however, supplanted the Inca religion of the Mother Earth. 'Why,' they ask, 'should the Virgin Mary drive out Pachamama?'

coloured pieces of wood which promise health, love or prosperity are on show beside others claiming more macabre effects. Dried llama foetuses are traditionally buried in the foundation of new buildings to bring good fortune to the occupants.

The markets also sell food: papaya milk-shakes, spiced chicken and rice, kebabs of ox heart with hot nut sauce, and fresh trout caught in nearby Lake Titicaca. The popular quarter of La Paz is, in effect, one huge market. The door of each house is a stall where something is for sale, perhaps a *humita* (mashed maize wrapped in leaves) or a glass of *pisco*, a lethal local brew. In the streets, Indians sit next to a handful of potatoes or a couple of onions, hoping to make a sale. It is a scene of colour and bustling activity, but it lacks the vocal banter associated with the marketplace; for the Indians never cry their wares or accost passers-by. They prefer to sit or stand in dignified silence waiting for custom to come to them.

The presidential palace, scene of so many coups, is closed to the public. The Museo Nacional de Arte, however, situated in the 18th-century Palacio de los Condes de Arana, provides a warmer welcome to visitors and contains interesting Indian sculpture. A larger collection of Chipaya Indian art is to be found at the Museo de Etnografía y Folklore, which displays weavings, musical instruments and other craftwork. Inca gold is on show at the Museo de Metales Preciosos. Ceramic and sculptural works of the Tiahuanaco culture are featured at the Museo Nacional de Arqueología. Of the many churches in La Paz – seen at their best when colourful Aymara weddings are taking place – the Iglesia de San Francisco, which was begun in 1549, is one of the finest.

Some 45 miles to the west of La Paz lies the ancient city of Tiahuanaco, or Tiwanaku, Bolivia's oldest and most important archaeological site. Archeologists may tell you that the site rivals Machu Picchu in importance, but the average visitor may find these ruins a little disappointing. As you approach the site, the ruins appear suddenly on the arid Altiplano, like a handful of stones, carelessly scattered and then forgotten. Open spaces, bounded by curious vertical stones carved as huge single pieces, contrast with the standing human

Villagers gather in the square by the church and dance the huayno *and* yaravi, *but all the ancient traditions and rites are tinged with an age-old melancholy.*

figures cut in stone and incised with delicate patterns. Because of a lack of funds, the site has never been properly dug, although it is likely that there are treasures here which would tell the whole story of a civilisation which emerged in about 1600 BC and had vanished by AD 700. These pre-Columbian megaliths form a ceremonial complex that was built between AD 200 and 700 beside the lake-shore, which subsequently receded. It is believed that the site conceals an ancient city that once had a population of 20,000 people.

Even the famous Gate of the Sun, in the Kalasasaya compound, is shrouded in mystery. Is it in fact a gate or was it once the capitol of some grander building? And what is the significance of the weeping sun-god, Viracocha, sculpted in the centre of the frieze? Does he cry in the foreknowledge that the stylised condors and jaguars which surround his head, and the priests who kneel at his side, will not be able to save his people from centuries of humiliation? Do the figures represent an Andean lunar calendar? Not far away is the Door of the Puma, surrounded by another pile of stones. But again, there are no guides to explain the significance of the sights, nor any clues from Aymara folklore. It is as if the Indians have completely lost touch with this relic of their past grandeur. Even the museum, established in a former hotel, leaves many questions unanswered.

The Valley of the Moon, an eerie landscape of canyons and rock pinnacles, is situated just a few miles from downtown La Paz. Alternatively, intrepid skiers keen to boast of having experienced the world's highest run should go to Chacaltaya, where slopes at 17,000 feet are reached by an elementary tow line. At this altitude, almost any exertion is exhausting.

Lake Titicaca

Lake Titicaca lies on the border between Bolivia and Peru at an altitude of 12,500 feet, making it the world's highest lake navigable by large vessels. The lake itself is immense, like a calm sea, and has its own microclimate which favours the growth of golden maize, barley, quinoa and potatoes on its densely populated shore. In such an arid environment, the fresh blue of the lake stands out with forbidding purity against the mountainous backdrop. Covering an area of about 3200 square miles, it has a number of islands and is fed by more than 25 rivers. In some parts the lake is 920 feet deep.

Trout were introduced in 1939 and now form a staple – though successive cholera scares have reduced the appetite for them. The Aymara fishermen in their brightly coloured ponchos and pointed *chullus* sail frail *balsas*, made from *totoras*, the reeds which grow on the banks. Together with modern steamboats, these traditional reed boats connect the lakeside settlements. Lake Titicaca is probably a relic of an inland sea that once covered much of the Altiplano, while in Indian mythology it was the womb of humankind and the birthplace of civilisation: it was from here that the sun-god rose above the waters to create the human race. On this sacred lake of the Incas are the islands of the Sun

and the Moon – legendary places covered in Inca ruins including those of the temple to Pajsi. It is no wonder that the Indians still revere the lake.

The most spectacular base for a visit to the lake is Copacabana, a small, sun-drenched town lying on the Peruvian border. Copacabana is a jewel of colonial Renaissance architecture, and for centuries was the destination of pilgrims in search of miracles wrought by the Black Virgin of the Lake, the *Virgen Moreña*. In February the Fiesta of the Virgin is celebrated, during which *balsas* are used to ferry the Virgin of the Sanctuary – made entirely of gold – across the lake. The

The miners of Catavi and Siglo XX celebrate the festival of the Copacabana Virgin by parading silver and tin objects before her.

In the mining town of Oruro, the carnival is called the Diablada. *Participants dance in honour of the Devil,* Supay, *and enact a parody of the Spanish conquest. Expressing the solidarity of the oppressed, this Indian dresses up in honour of the blacks who perished in the silver-mines at Potosí.*

celebration involves a great deal of singing and dancing and, as the mellow notes of the panpipes float out over the water, you can hear Indian music at its most authentic. You can also witness traditional dances here: the *sicuri*, the *kabyo, zapateado, huacatorri* and the *cueca*. Men and women will dance until they drop and there is no more drink to revive them. The music is not joyous, but has a sadness which seems to reflect the people's dark past.

At Copacabana, the Indians also venerate an older god, called Ekeko. He is celebrated on January 24, during the festival of *Alacitas feria*. This cheerful little figure, a symbol of prosperity and happiness, was a household god in pre-Inca times. Today, on Alacitas day, all the markets of Bolivia resemble Lilliput. Indians buy miniatures of all sorts of objects which they then offer to Ekeko in the hope that he will reward the righteous with life-size versions of the same things.

Copacabana is also the point from which the islands of the Sun and Moon may be visited. The larger island of the Sun is inhabited; it is crossed by a network of paths between Inca ruins, and is also the site of one of the most sacred Inca relics, the sacred rock where creation began. According to myth, the rain god

Caricatures poke fun at Spanish nobles and their wives at the Diablada.

Devilry in Oruro

Year after year, the *Diablada* is performed at Oruro on the Saturday before Ash Wednesday: a ritual whose dominant theme is the Spanish conquest of Latin America and the cruelty of the colonial powers.

Leading the processions are two figures representing a bear and a condor, whose task is to clear the way for the masqueraders behind them. Then comes a luridly costumed quartet, representing Satan and Lucifer (regarded as separate figures), the Archangel Michael and the Devil's wife and arch-temptress China Supay. Behind them come a mass of extravagently masked followers.

The procession winds its way through Oruro's thronged streets – where *gringos* (foreigners) should tread warily, since they are usually the butt of numerous practical jokes – and ends in the city's football stadium. Here, the masqueraders perform the ritual dances for which the *Diablada* is famous.

The martyr Atahualpa dances with his executioner Pizarro. When he meets his end, the emperor dies with dignity, refusing the gospels and urging his people to fight the white oppression. For their part, the Spaniards are represented in absurd costumes and masks. Half demons, and half comic puppets, the *pelucones* cause great hilarity among the descendants of their victims. Blacks, too, take part in the dance – or rather Indians posing as blacks – reaffirming the solidarity of the oppressed.

The *moreñada* is danced to commemorate the blacks who were sent to the silver-mines at Potosí and died within a matter of weeks. Only the Aymaras have the constitution to work at that altitude. The song of *ñustas* is also performed. In this, virgins, dedicated to the sun, mourn the death of Atahualpa, the beloved Inca who was taken prisoner and strangled by Pizarro.

A performance of the *relato* ends the procession. This dance, created by a Catholic priest at the turn of the century, tells the story of St Michael's conquest of evil. The devils cast aside their masks and bow down before the Virgin: a Christian ending to a pagan festival.

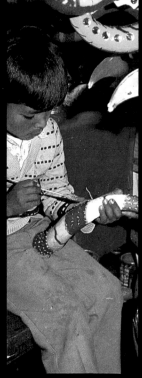

Viracocha and the very first Incas – Manco Kapac and his sister-wife Mama Huaca – appeared on this spot and promptly departed for Cuzco to found the empire.

Oruro, to the south of La Paz, is the only other significant city in the Altiplano. This is the home of another great traditional festival, the *Diablada* (Dance of the Devils). Not only is it a wonderful spectacle, but it also gives an insight into the lives of the Aymaras. The brightly coloured plaster masks which represent the face of the Devil, and the velvet capes and embroidered white satin costumes, all date back to Inca times. In this ritual, which takes place a week before the beginning of Lent, the Indians act out their history. More than this, it is a celebration of Tio, the two-faced spirit – sometimes good, sometimes evil – who lives in the mines.

Oruro is a dour mining town and its miners, who spend most of their lives underground scratching for tin, welcome the opportunity of celebrating Tio in the sun. Spectators watch the procession of multicoloured devils and *pelucones*, Indian caricatures of Spanish colonial officials, and think of the mines. For these are

truly horrific places. In 1949, the miners had the temerity to strike; the Bolivian army was sent in and more than 4000 workers were killed. Even today, labour laws are honoured in the breach rather than the observance, and Indians may spend upwards of 10 hours a day underground.

Nowhere are the past horrors of mining more powerfully evoked than in Potosí. Situated beside the Cerro Rico (rich hill), one of the most abundant ore mountains, Potosí is the source of much of the world's silver, as well as tin, tungsten and copper. Today, Potosí also manufactures mining and electrical equipment. By 1650, a century after silver had first been discovered

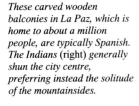

These carved wooden balconies in La Paz, which is home to about a million people, are typically Spanish. The Indians (right) generally shun the city centre, preferring instead the solitude of the mountainsides.

here, Potosí had a population of 160,000: it was the largest city in the Americas and one of the most important commercial centres in the world. Today it is a shadow of its former self, another chapter in Bolivia's history.

Before the Spanish discovered Cerro Rico, in 1544, the Inca Huayna Capac had begun to mine it. According to legend, however, he abandoned the enterprise when he heard a thunderous noise and a great voice from the mountain booming: 'The Lord reserves these treasures for he who is to come.' His obedience was symptomatic of the South American Indians' extraordinary passivity. Perhaps they knew the Spanish would arrive one day,

and saw little point in resisting the inevitable. For two centuries Potosí's wealth kept the Spanish monarchy on its throne, but at appalling cost. As many as 8 million Indian and African slaves are believed to have died underground.

When the Spanish found the mine, they forced the Indians to excavate the *cerro* which, during the colonial period, yielded billions of pounds' worth of silver. The hill has long since been mined out, and Potosí is now just a large rural Indian town, with no more than the echoes of a fabulous past. There are churches with elaborate baroque façades, and private homes with carved wooden balconies which look down on narrow,

winding streets. The mines can be visited and there are many fine museums, including the *Casa de la Moneda* which served the Spanish empire as a mint, fortress and prison after it was built in 1572.

In this city of contrasts, some of the residents, dressed in fine, handwoven woollen garments, carry on the cultural traditions of their Quechua Indian ancestors. The others, wearing modern dress, are probably the descendants of the Indians and the Spaniards, who were drawn to the city by the lure of silver. They can be seen mingling in the markets, attending mass in the baroque churches, walking through the narrow streets or sitting in the city squares. They are bound by an understanding of the Quechua language but divided by cultural and class barriers.

Despite the harsh climate and poverty that abounds in a city situated 13,000 feet above sea level, the people of Potosí are cheerful and hospitable. Indian women wearing multi-layered skirts can be seen walking the streets or selling *tawa tawas, chambergos* or *sopaipillas* – delicious sweet pastries.

Life in Potosí today is hard. The land around the city is some of the most arid in the Altiplano. Nothing grows and even the llama is nowhere to be seen. But the people live somehow. The mines still operate, but these days they extract tin rather than silver, and there are the *palliras*, women who spend all day on the side of the *cerro*, silently crushing pieces of ore with hammers, hoping they will contain fragments of silver, tin or tungsten. For this is today's pitiful share of the legendary riches of Potosí.

The subtropical paradise hours from La Paz and the arid Altiplano. The yungas *(valleys) are fertile and have a constant spring-like climate.*

Butch Cassidy and the Sundance Kid

Imagine you are travelling northwards to the Bolivian capital by train from Argentina: after the frontier, the first town of importance is Villazón. Wheezing along its bumpy tracks, your train climbs slowly up through the Andes, passing stations whose platforms are as crowded as any street-market. There are sellers of *api* (a purple, maize-based drink), *chicha* beer, *empanadas* (meat pies) and delicious stews so powerfully spiced that they bring tears to the eyes.

The mining town of Tupiza brings rather different associations. Some 50 miles to its north-west, at the head of a spectacular canyon, lies the dusty village of San Vicente where – according to the most probable version of the story, at least – a shoot-out took place in November 1908 between a Bolivian military patrol and two North American ne'er-do-wells, Robert Leroy Parker and Harry Longabaugh. Two days earlier, the Americans, better known to history as the bank and train robbers Butch Cassidy and the Sundance Kid, had held up the payroll convoy of a local mining company. It was to be their last successful operation. Both were killed in the shoot-out and are said to be buried in an unmarked grave in San Vicente's cemetery.

After Tupiza the tracks pass through the regions where gold was once mined. Stretching out to the west is the Salar de Uyuni, a massive dry salt lake containing millions of tons of edible salt; it is the remains of a far greater prehistoric salt lake that probably covered much of the country. A visit to the flats involves getting off the train at Uyuni. The saltpan has a number of settlements along its shores, where locals make a living extracting salt. Surviving islands, such as the Isla del Pescado, have extraordinary cactus vegetation, the only greenery in this lunar landscape. Back on the train heading northwards, the tracks pass close to the Lago Poopó, where pink flamingoes cluster. Lago Uru Uru, which is situated just south of Oruro and conected to Lago Poopó, also provides a splendid view of its flamingoes.

Fertile terraces

A subtropical region known as the Yungas sweeps down from the Altiplano to Bolivia's steaming Amazon basin, forming the natural transition zone between the chilly uplands and the sweltering plain. The contrast with the high plateau could not be more extreme. The fertile soil of these valleys supports giant maize, coffee, cacao and exotic fruits on ancient Inca terraces. The Yungas are considerably warmer because of their lower altitude, while their northern part has a humid subtropical climate. The southern Yungas have the most pleasant climate in all Bolivia, and offer fine opportunities for hiking.

This is the home of the Quechua Indians, the natural descendants of the Incas, and hence, it is said, of the Sun: the inheritors of a civilisation based on the cultivation of maize and on social order. Their appearance is very different from that of the Aymaras of the Altiplano. Their undyed woollen clothes are cleaner; the men wear knee-length breeches and flat hats, and the women have wavy hair. They are a handsome people: small, but with fine physiques, reminiscent of the statuettes at Tanagra. They have gentle faces and speak their melodious language in hushed tones.

Like the Aymaras, the Quechuas were freed from *pongaje,* or serfdom, by the agrarian reforms of the 1950s, although they still work their tiny sections of land alongside the *haciendas* of their erstwhile bosses. The plots might be small, but the land is generous and produces enough maize and fruit to ensure that the community is well fed. The village of Coroico, situated some 50 miles from La Paz and at an altitude of 5000 feet, is a perfect example of Yunga life. Its spectacular position, breathtaking views and opportunities to hike along Inca trails dotted with the occasional ruin make Coroico a favourite with travellers.

The owners of the surviving plantations belong to the old Creole aristocracy and, for the most part, live in the delightful city of Sucre, which was founded by the Spaniard Pedro de Anzures in 1538. Sucre is known as *La Ciudad Blanca* (the White City) for its cleanliness and for the fact that the houses and churches are whitewashed every year by government edict. Long isolated from the rest of Bolivia, Sucre has retained much of its colonial heritage and is essentially 18th century in character. It is perpetually bathed in sunlight, which illuminates the blue-and-white Spanish tiles of the patios and the dark wooden balconies, highlighting the flowers which grow everywhere. The cumulative effect of its churches, ancient mansions and museums is dazzling. Still the legal and judicial capital of Bolivia, Sucre stands at an elevation of 9150 feet. The city was known during the colonial period as Chuquisaca, and its name was changed to Sucre only in 1840 to honour Antonio José de Sucre, leader of the independence struggle.

Sucre is a city of great refinement and culture. The University of San Xavier was founded in 1624 and was the font of the liberal idealism which gave birth to the first cry for independence in South America. The city still buzzes with students. Buildings that date from early colonial times are everywhere, housing priceless carvings and collections of paintings, furniture and religious figures adorned with gold and jewelled robes. It was in the legislative palace that the declaration of independence was signed on August 6, 1825. The building, also known as the Casa de la Libertad, is now a museum with a number of exhibits from General Sucre's revolutionary era.

The 17th-century cathedral on the Plaza 25 de Mayo has a fine tower decorated with statues of the apostles, while more gorgeously adorned religious artefacts are on view in the Museo de la Iglesia and the chapel of the Virgen de Guadelupe. The Convento and Museo la Recoleta, situated on a hill south-east of the city centre, offer wonderful views and the tranquility of a Franciscan retreat.

Cochabamba, north of Sucre, is the city of eternal spring. Nestling at the foot of the Tunari – although still at an altitude of more than 8000 feet – the city is the centre of Bolivia's richest agricultural region, and is an important alpaca craft centre and holiday resort. It has a population of more than 300,000 and vies with Santa Cruz for the distinction of being Bolivia's second city. As in Sucre, all the buildings are whitewashed, dazzling in the brilliant sunlight. It has a splendid park and gardens, and its tree-lined avenues and the patios of its colonial buildings are festooned with countless colourful flowers and plants.

Founded in 1574 by the Spanish, Cochabamba soon became the granary of the empire, though today few relics of that era survive. Perhaps its most distinctive monument is the Palacio de Portales – a tribute to the riches and extravagance of Bolivia's cruellest tin baron, Simón Patiño. The palace, built around 1920 by one of the world's ten richest men and designed by European architects, was constructed entirely from imported items, brought at huge expense from Europe. The building was never inhabited, and now houses a museum and cultural centre. Simón Patiño built another palace at Pairumani, south-west of the city. Called the Villa Albina, it bears mute witness to Patiño's extraordinary extravagance.

The chola *of Cochabamba – of mixed white and Quechua blood – wears a top hat* (left), *whitewashed and hardened with lime. Five centuries on, the helmet of the* conquistadores *has also been incorporated into Indian costume* (above).

The llama is the only real companion of the Aymaras. It serves as a beast of burden and, with its capacity to withstand cold and hunger, is one of the few animals on earth which could thrive on the Altiplano.

The wild east

The valleys of the Yungas spread south into Bolivia's tropical lowlands. Known as the Oriente, this vast area of jungle, swampland and rough pasture accounts for more than 70 per cent of Bolivia's total land mass. It is little known, sparsely populated, enticing and dangerous.

The northern part of the Oriente – the provinces of Beni and Pando – was developed extensively in the 17th and 18th centuries by Jesuit priests to provide European markets with tropical fruits, nuts and dried beef. After the Jesuits had been expelled, however, their plantations fell into decay and roads to the outside world became overgrown and impassable.

Reyes, the only town of any consequence in the north of the Oriente, can best be reached by air. Here you will see herds of zebus, hump-backed cows with hides that appear too big for their frames. They were introduced to the area from India by the Jesuits. The people, too, seem incongruous. They are for the most part tall, white Andalusians – moustachioed men, with white hats and gun belts, and elegant women.

To the south of Reyes lies Beni and the end of civilisation. Beyond is the jungle, the heart of the forest. Here, Indians and mixed-race locals collect latex from the trunks of rubber-producing *heveas* trees. They are engulfed by clouds of insects, attracted by the moisture of their sweat-covered bodies. Enormous blue butterflies as big as a hand flutter in the half light. There are snakes, too, including the massive, grotesque *sícuri* which lies by the river banks, waiting for an unsuspecting calf to come along; the snake will swallow the beast whole, then lie back for several weeks slowly digesting the succulent flesh. Even the plants are predatory. Place a finger on certain blossoms, and you will feel the flower tremble: it is a carnivorous flower expecting to entice an unwary insect into its deadly trap.

The southern region of the Oriente centres on Santa Cruz, a city founded in 1561 by a Spanish captain named Nuflo de Chávez. Forty years ago this was a jungle outpost where oxen pulled carts through mud streets. Today, however, it has mushroomed into a sweltering city of more than half a million people and is the vanguard of Bolivia's economic revival. Modern office blocks are sprouting up alongside traditional adobe homes with curved tiled roofs. The reason for this dramatic transformation is quite simple: there is oil and natural gas here.

Santa Cruz is a brash, noisy, Wild West sort of town that really took off in the 1950s, when road and rail links first joined it with La Paz to the west and Brazil to the east. Now Bolivia's second largest city, Santa Cruz has little to remind visitors of the past and its links are more cosmopolitan. Immigrants or businessmen from Japan and the United States mingle with those who have moved here from the Mennonite colonies of Paraguay. Because Santa Cruz is one of the most important points in the cocaine trading route, drug money has severely tainted the city.

Since the department of Santa Cruz borders Brazil to the east, there has always been a strong Brazilian influence here. This is especially noticeable during the pre-Lenten Carnival. Beautiful women in elaborate costumes, similar to those seen in Rio de Janeiro at Carnival time, parade through the streets, and the town is caught up in an orgy of music, drinking and dancing. The weekend after Carnival, the same women, their identities still concealed behind masks, frequent the city's bars and nightclubs, a token revenge against their perennially unfaithful husbands.

Barefoot and hungry, these little Aymara girls are destined for a life of true hardship. Their people have known nothing better for centuries.

Chile

From the desert of Atacama in the north to the wind-swept wilds of Cape Horn in the south, Chile stretches ribbon-like down South America's south-western flank. In between, it encompasses mountains, fjords, lakes and wooded islands, all of a haunting beauty. For a long time, its exemplary political stability earned it the nickname the 'England of South America'. But that record was broken during a turbulent experiment with socialism, followed by savage dictatorship, in the 1970s and 80s. It has settled down since then and boasts one of the fastest-growing economies in the continent.

Copper is Chile's most important natural resource. Chilean craftsmen fashion jewellery from the metal, using decorative themes which date back to pre-Columbian times.

El Teniente is the largest underground copper-mine in the world. The red ore is found in the majestic Andes cordillera. Since the price of saltpetre has collapsed, copper has become Chile's biggest export.

Previous page: This Andean scene from the far north of Chile could equally well be set in Bolivia, Peru, the north of Argentina or Ecuador. For all share the same arid terrain, the same flocks, the same stone enclosures (pircas), and the same types of hats.

A Corner of Europe in South America

Chile may be a distant nation, but it provided the world with one of the seminal political dramas of our age: the violent overthrow of the world's first democratically elected Marxist government outside Europe, by the right-wing dictator General Augusto Pinochet. The American-aided coup d'état in September 1973, in which the leftist President Salvador Allende died in Santiago's bombed-out Moneda palace, inspired extraordinary passions that Chile is still working hard to forget. But since 1990 – when the return of democracy brought an end to 17 years of military rule during which over 2000 people were killed, 40,000 arrested and human rights were abused countless times – Chile has wrought a miracle, healing itself and growing with extraordinary speed. It is a tribute to the depth and generosity of the Chilean spirit that reconciliation and forgiveness have largely washed away those dark years.

With good reason, Chileans are passionate about their extraordinary but captivating ribbon of a country, once described as a sword hanging from the belt of South America. Chile has captivated the business community too: economically, this country has more in common with the fast-growing countries on the other side of the Pacific than with its problematic South American neighbours. While its neighbours suffer from inflation and stagnation, Chile's chief problem has been administering its economic growth of over 8 per cent a year and the numerous foreign investors that this has attracted.

Dominated by the backbone of the Andes, Chile is still rattled by periodic earthquakes. It is astonishingly beautiful, with landscapes ranging from glaciers to desert, and from forbidding mountains or volcanoes to lush, vine-clad valleys reminiscent of rural France. The Chileans may be few – the population is only 13 million – and their country may have an average width of only 110 miles, but Chile runs deep in other ways. It does, after all, stretch more than 2600 miles down the Pacific coast from Peru to the southern tip of the continent at Cape Horn, including the larger part of Tierra del Fuego, an island separated from the mainland by the Strait of Magellan.

Chile possesses some extraordinary islands, too: Easter Island is situated in the south-eastern Pacific Ocean, about 2300 miles from the coast, and is famous for its giant neolithic statues. The mysterious island's Dutch discoverers called it Paaseiland (Easter Island) to commemorate the day it was sighted. Alone in the middle of more than a million square miles of ocean, it is known as *Rapa Nui* (the navel of the world) by its 2000 Polynesian residents. There, against a background of sumptuous tropical vegetation at the foot of the volcano Rano Raraku, stand the *moais*, the giant stone

The condor, the world's biggest flying bird, is a symbol of freedom to the countries of the Andes.

Copper is found in its pure state in the mines of Chile. This is unusual, for it is normally mixed with other minerals to form oxides, sulphides and carbonates.

statues which have intrigued visitors to the island for centuries. Despite the many volumes that have been written about these 45 square miles of volcanic rock – including a work by the Norwegian explorer Thor Heyerdahl – the statues and the culture from which they sprang remain enigmas.

More fantasy than mystery is attached to its other offshore dependency, the Juan Fernandez Islands. It was on one of these – now known as Robinson Crusoe Island – that a Scotsman, Alexander Selkirk, was abandoned in 1681. His story, published after his rescue in 1684, provided Daniel Defoe with the source material for *Robinson Crusoe*.

Chile may look like a cartographer's afterthought (indeed, one legend says that when God had completed the labour of the Creation and lay down to sleep, he threw all the surplus natural wonders over the Andes to form the country) but it has been long in the making. Chile was once part of the Inca empire, though it had earlier been ruled by the Araucans, a proud, warlike Indian people.

When the *conquistadores*, accustomed to Inca passivity, moved into Chile from Peru, they were surprised by the ferocity of the Araucans. Their resistance, and the absence of gold, might have discouraged the Spanish colonists if Chile had not controlled the western approaches to the strategic southern straits discovered by Magellan in 1520. Don Pedro de Valdivia, who founded Santiago in 1541 and colonised much of the fertile heartland, was killed by Mapuche Indians who almost forced out the Spanish. However, they themselves were eventually driven back behind the Bío-Bío river, which then marked the boundary between the northern peoples, who had been overpowered by the Incas and the Spanish, and the indomitable Araucan Indians in the south.

Spanish tenure of its Chilean colony was never tranquil, and in 1811 scattered uprisings erupted into a full-scale war of independence. Chilean-born Creoles had declared their autonomy in 1810 but it was not until they were united by Bernardo O'Higgins, the illegitimate son of an Irish-born viceroy of Lima, that they became a military threat. In an extraordinary march across the Andes, O'Higgins led troops from Mendoza to the central valley of Chile to attack the Spanish after joining together with rebel forces under the Argentinian José de San Martín. After the final defeat of the Spanish forces there in 1818, O'Higgins was elected supreme director, which he remained until ousted by conservative landowners in 1823. The Spanish, meanwhile, retreated to the southern island of Chiloé, which they kept until 1826 as their last outpost on the South American continent.

Chile's next conflict was the War of the Pacific (1879–83), in which it defeated Bolivia and Peru for control of the rich mineral deposits in the Atacama Desert. Chile's expanded territory cut Bolivia off from the sea. It's returning armies were then deployed in genocidal battles against the Indians in the far south, whose land was colonised by German settlers.

The legalisation of the Communist party in 1952 and other social reforms led to the 1970 election victory for Salvador Allende, who initiated a chaotic Chilean road to socialism, which involved antagonising large landowners, mine owners, bankers and, importantly, US business interests. General Augusto Pinochet, who had been Allende's trusted army commander, set about reversing his reforms by means of a *laissez-faire* economic miracle that won over the middle classes, but left almost half the population in considerable hardship.

Pinochet, already leader of the military junta, became president in 1980 under new constitutional rules, but in

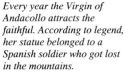

Every year the Virgin of Andacollo attracts the faithful. According to legend, her statue belonged to a Spanish soldier who got lost in the mountains.

1988 the people of Chile rejected his plan to rule for another eight years and the opposition united behind Patricio Aylwin, a moderate Christian Democrat who took power in 1990. Aylwin has had to reconcile demands for justice from frustrated victims of human rights abuse and the looming presence of Pinochet, still in command of a largely unrepentant army.

Hidden behind the Andes

Although the Andean countries were home to a fifth of the continent's indigenous peoples at the time of the first European contacts, Chile is conspicuously less 'Indian' than Bolivia or Peru. In fact, it is the most European of these nations, with a clean, tidy lifestyle

In the north of Chile, magical Virgins are commonplace. This procession in Andacollo, for example, has its origins in both the Catholic faith and the ancient traditions of the Incas.

Fantasy and folklore, rather than tradition, dominate the way of life in northern Chile. This little girl's bowler hat is typical of those adopted by cholas in the 19th century in imitation of the British engineers who had come to build the railways.

and an efficient infrastructure that seems decades ahead of its neighbours. Perhaps it is Chile's physical isolation behind the Andes that has contributed to a sense of clannishness. Spanish and Indian are not, however, the only races to be found in contemporary Chile, which was a magnet for European immigrants in the last century. Chile's navy was formed by an Englishman, Lord Cochrane, while the country's greatest writer and historian, Don Benjamín Vicuña Mackenna, was half Scot. Three recent presidents have been of Italian, Swiss and German origin. Traces of these migrant cultures are still strong: parts of the Lake District resemble Bavaria, while Serbians and other Slavs have settled in both the Atacama Desert in the north and in the far south.

Around two-thirds of Chile's people are *mestizos* (of mixed Indian and white ancestry), but there are still about 150,000 descendants of the original Araucanian Indians living in the forests south of the Bío-Bío river. The fighting spirit of the Araucans probably accounts for the fact that the majority of Chileans are of Spanish descent; in the early days, few Chilean Indians intermarried with the colonists, unlike their more docile neighbours to the north. Even today – although there is

Indian blood to be found in the working classes – mixed Spanish and Indian blood is rare in the middle and upper classes.

For centuries, the lands south of the Bío-Bío represented a no-go area not only for the Spanish but also for the *criollos*, the Chilean whites who had freed themselves from Hispanic rule. White men settled in the region at their peril: the city of Angol, for instance, was destroyed by the Indians no fewer than seven times between 1552 and 1802.

At the turn of the last century the last revolutionary chief of the southern Araucan Indians, Caupolicán, had

The small stone houses of this arid, wind-swept land have thatched roofs. An entire family will live in a single, windowless room, blackened by smoke. At night, they sleep on the bare earth.

The sanctuary of the Virgin of the Rocks in Quebrada de Azapa. It is said that, in the 16th century, this Virgin saved a shepherd couple from wild animals.

expansionist dreams. Having led his army across the Andes into Argentina in the south, he travelled north up through Argentinian Patagonia, across the pampas and right up to the gates of Buenos Aires. The Argentinian Araucans were soon driven out but on the Chilean side their kinsmen fared rather better, and their culture is still very much alive. For the most part, they live in their own villages, albeit in some poverty. The sight of them hanging around street corners, dressed in Levis and trainers and listening to transistor radios, does not mean that they have lost touch with their old ways. It is just that their customs are not designed as tourist attractions.

Although prouder, and in some ways more open, than the Indian peoples to the north – the Quechuas and the Aymaras – they are reluctant to discuss spiritual matters with outsiders, let alone make an exhibition of them. For instance, the *nguillatún*, the annual festival where Araucans meet around the *rehue* (altar) to offer their prayers to God, is a sacred affair. In their shamanic religion, the world is pervaded by good and evil spirits, and the *machi* (sorceress) acts as a bridge between heaven and earth: she wears a black-and-white poncho with a geometric design representing the staircase by which she climbs, in a trance, to the

As you travel farther south, the desert gives way to fertile valleys where people grow olives, oranges, vegetables and very sweet grapes from which they make pisco, *a type of brandy.*

very ear of God to ask him to have pity on his people.

Over 80 per cent of Chile's population is now urban; with more than a third of the country's population, about 4.5 million people, living in or around Santiago. Another 15 per cent live in 11 provincial capitals, the most important of which are Valparaíso and Concepción. Life in the *callampas* (mushroom squatter towns) – also named *poblaciones* – which stretch from the outskirts of Santiago almost to the foot of the snow-capped mountain range behind the capital, is dignified but harsh: it is easy to see how Allende's brand of activism once struck a chord here. It is in these areas

that the Catholic church is still most deeply rooted: during the darkest Pinochet days, its *Vicaría de la Solidaridad* was almost the only beacon of hope.

The extraordinary charm and vitality of the Chileans is reflected in the richness of their artistic life, and especially in their literary prowess. The poets Gabriela Mistral and Pablo Neruda both won Nobel prizes. Neruda ranks as one of the greatest Spanish-American poets and one of the few to have achieved worldwide recognition. A lifelong socialist who sided with the Republicans during the Spanish Civil War, the writer, diplomat and senator died only a few days after the

coup d'état that overthrew his friend Salvador Allende.

Andean popular music, which is characterised by panpipe-like flutes and the mandolin, can be heard everywhere and has been pressed into political service. The cowboys (*huasos*) provide much of the entertainment at traditional Chilean rodeos or fiestas. Their *cueca* dances and music represent a blending of many of the European traditions brought over by migrants, with relics of the older Mapuche traditions. The rodeo is a favourite form of entertainment in Chile: an opportunity for the *huasos* to show off.

The *huasos*, from the central plains, are similar to the *gauchos* of Argentina – semi-nomadic horsemen of mixed race, who are famous for their *machismo* and have traditionally worked as hired hands on the cattle ranches. Today, many of them have found a more agreeable and profitable existence as rodeo cowboys. The *huaso* is more than a rural anachronism, however; he is very much a symbol of Chilean manhood, an ideal to which ordinary young Chilean men aspire. The *huasos* do indeed cut a dash with their brightly coloured jackets and tight trousers decorated from the knee down with long fringes, vividly striped waist-length ponchos, silver spurs and straight-brimmed hats tied under the chin.

Three countries in one land

For historical, geographic and climatic reasons, Chile is usually divided into three regions. In the north, there is a dry, rainless desert with arid plains and barren mountains. The central region consists of a vast fertile valley, which lies between the Andes and the coastal plateau and stretches 500 miles from Coquimbo in the north to Concepcíon in the south. This region enjoys a mild winter and a warm, dry, summer climate, and is the heartland of Chile's agricultural, commercial and cultural life, as well as home to around 90 per cent of its citizens.

The southern region stretches from Concepción south to Tierra del Fuego. Its coastline is a network of fjords, islands and peninsulas, with forests and a sprinkling of

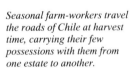

In the very south of Chile, this climbing plant, the copihue, winds itself around the trees. Its bright pink flowers add a splash of colour to the dark, damp forests.

Seasonal farm-workers travel the roads of Chile at harvest time, carrying their few possessions with them from one estate to another.

lakes inland. A region of great beauty, it suffers from a harsh climate of fierce winds, rain and cold. It is still home to the Araucan Indians, the only people tough enough, or perhaps stubborn enough, to live in such an inhospitable environment. Farther south, Chile lays claim to a strip of Antarctica – territory which is also claimed by Great Britain. At its tips, the largest of which is situated on King George Island (which can be reached year-round by aircraft), families of colonists carry on a bizarre frontier existence that the government believes will strengthen its territorial claim.

Similarly, if viewed east to west, the country divides into three sections: the Andes; the Central Valley, which is divided by mountain spurs and rivers carrying run-off from the Andes; and a coastal escarpment 2500 feet high, which ends in steep cliffs along the Pacific coast. The best-known mountain ranges are in the central region and include volcanoes, such as Tupungato

(22,310 feet), Maipo (17,459 feet), and the second-highest peak in the Western Hemisphere, Ojos del Salado (22,516 feet).

The wealth of the deserts

The Atacama Desert of northern Chile is the source of much of the country's wealth. It is rich in copper and other mineral resources. Chuquicamata, for example, is the biggest open-cast copper-mine in the world. Chile has overtaken the United States as the world's leading producer of copper and its mines, nationalised by the Allende government, remain largely under state control. Iron ore, gold, silver, nitrates, lithium, molybdenum (a metallic element used in steel alloys and various fertilisers and dyes), and other minerals are exported too. At one time, northern Chile was also the world's leading producer of saltpetre. Now that substance is manufactured rather than mined, and the desert is littered with ghost towns that are monuments to a once-vibrant industry.

The desert also conceals the ruins of much older civilisations of the Inca and pre-Inca periods. The inhabitants here still speak the Aymara language; indeed, in Aymara, Chile means 'distant country'. If modern life has left its scars from mining, the ancient cultures have left more harmonious signs of their passing: huge designs of men, gods and animals. The largest design, the Giant of Atacama, is 360 feet long, while hundreds of others are laid out on the hillside. The most distinctive are to be seen around Iquique.

Chile begins at Arica, the northern city where rain never falls. It was from Arica that the wealth of Bolivia's silver-mines was shipped out, though today the port is better known for its fishing fleet, and the warm waters that draw holidaymakers to its beaches.

These fishermen, surrounded by pelicans, have come from the port of Antofagasta. Thanks to the Humboldt Current, the waters off Chile are cold and fish is abundant.

The fishing port of Valparaíso, once a refuge for corsairs and whalers, was the busiest harbour on the Pacific coast until the Californian gold rush.

The town has tunnels and fortresses built during the Spanish colonial era as defence against pirates hungry for silver. Two other extraordinary reminders of Africa's past are the church of San Marcos, a prefabricated iron structure designed by the French engineer Gustave Eiffel – of Eiffel Tower fame – and the customs house, which he also built.

Iquique, to the south, is a city with dramatic views over the Pacific Ocean; its bustle is guaranteed by its duty-free status for shoppers. It has many luxurious mansions and public buildings built on mining wealth in the last century, but the chief attractions lie inland in the Pica valley. Here the Festival of La Tirana, held in the middle of July, is one of the most distinctive cultural events of the region. The Pica valley itself is one of those miraculously fertile oases in the desert, where mango and orange trees are to be found.

La Tirana is named after a tyrannical Inca princess named Ñusta Huillac, who appears to have been little loved by her own people. But she fell passionately in love with a Portuguese prisoner who, with the intervention of the Carmelite Virgin, then converted her to his Catholic religion. Later, however, Spanish soldiers killed both the princess and her Portuguese admirer, and it is the fate of these tragic lovers that is

A network of funiculars climb the 41 hills of Valparaíso. These particular lifts climb up Polanco Hill, from where there is a panoramic view over the town and harbour.

The city of Valparaíso once stretched right out into the sea so that, until the middle of the last century, ships could drop anchor right in the city centre.

The Chilean huaso *protects his legs with leather gaiters* (corralijas), *rather than high boots.*

Like the Argentinian gaucho, *the Chilean* huaso *spends his life on horseback. He is a symbol of independent manhood in a country where machismo is the order of the day.*

celebrated in the festival. It is one of Chile's most famous, and brings huge numbers of visitors to enjoy the sight of dancers wearing red ornate masks topped with golden horns.

The port city of Antofagasta is perched on top of the coastal escarpment in this 700-mile long northern region. It is from here that ore from the mines of the Atacama is shipped. Founded by a miner in 1845, Antofagasta is a progressive city with beautiful plazas (one with a handsome clock tower donated by the city's sizeable British community) and parks that defy the desert environment. The very existence of these parks is, in fact, a direct by-product of the region's mining tradition. Over the centuries, European ships which came

A cattle ranch in the land of huasos. *The dark, heavy clouds are more evocative of the south where it rains constantly. Chilean poet Pablo Neruda wrote: 'About the days and years of my childhood I shall say first that the only unforgettable character for me was the rain . . . I think the art of raining has been lost. It exercised a subtle, terrible power over my native Araucania.'*

In the village of Panimavida, craftswomen make tiny baskets, figures and flowers *from horsehair and from vegetable fibres from the roots of poplar trees.*

to the port unloaded their ballast of earth on the quayside and, as a result, Antofagasta's gardens now flourish on Irish, German and Japanese soil. Those ships took away guano, a natural fertiliser made from bird droppings, which is an important part of the Chilean economy.

Chile's fishing industry excels, thanks to the Humboldt Current which sweeps icy but nutrient-rich waters up from Antarctica. Abundant fish stocks, including the traditional Chilean favourite *congrio* (the conger eel) as well others such as marlin and swordfish, attract game fishermen. But working fishermen thrive too, and in Antofagasta each year they hold a festival on June 29 in honour of St Peter, their patron. A launch carries an image of the saint out to the harbour break-

water, and there among the assembled fishing vessels the day's first catch is blessed.

Nothing grows in the Atacama Desert, the driest place on earth. But further south there are fertile valleys, which are watered by the rivers Copiapó and Huasco. These are the fringes of Chile's rich agricultural belt, where a wide range of fruit, notably wine grapes, are cultivated. Thanks to the know-how of its European migrants, Chile's high-quality wines are making inroads on world markets.

There is animal life here, too: llama-like vicuñas, wild cats and condors, and an abundance of humming birds. Southwards towards La Serena, on the road to the Chilean heartland, the farmland is richer: market sellers

display wonderful assortments of produce – papayas, mangos, magnificent asparagus and *chirimoyas* (white figs) – alongside ceramic animals known as *diaguitas* and *atacameñas*. The white figs are a local delicacy and the pottery is a legacy of times when the region was under Inca influence. The area has another claim to fame: more days of sunshine than anywhere else in the world, and air which is almost totally free from pollution. It was for this reason that astronomers chose La Serena as the location for the Cerro Tololo

Sailors' lairs in Valparaíso

Central Chile begins southwards along the coast from Coquimbo. Until the Californian gold rush and the growth of places such as San Francisco, the city of Valparaíso was the busiest port on the Pacific, and it still has the feeling of a frontier town. Situated on the coast about 70 miles from the capital, Valparaíso has an illustrious past, though architectural memories of its status as the country's financial and commercial

This craft centre at Huerto Cisnes encourages the revival of traditional crafts threatened by modern manufacturing techniques.

In Valparaíso – the Valley of Paradise – the houses are painted in bright colours, giving the city a naïve quality which is reflected in the crafts of the region.

Observatory, which is considered to be one of the three finest astronomical installations in the world.

Coquimbo, La Serena's seaport, boasts the caves where Sir Francis Drake is supposed to have hidden treasure seized on the Spanish Main, and also a steel church designed by Eiffel. The town is the scene of several colourful religious celebrations, notably the pilgrimage to the Virgin of nearby Andacollo. Legend has it that the statue belonged to a Spanish soldier who got lost in the mountains. But then the mountains abound with stories of virgins, lost and found. Here in the north the most important festivals celebrated are those of the Virgins of Guadeloupe and of the Candelaria.

capital have largely been swept away by earthquakes.

Old Valparaíso must have been a sailor's dream, for until the last century, ships could literally cast anchor beside the seamen's homes. So close did the sea come that the area now covered by the Plaza Victoria was once covered by water; and stories abound of shipwrecks on this very spot. The port itself is a maze of narrow streets and underground taverns, once a refuge of pirates and whalers, and still a place to be approached with a degree of caution. English pirates, including Richard Hawkins and Sir Francis Drake, repeatedly attacked the city after its founding in 1536. More recently, the British sailor Lord Cochrane came to Chile's aid, assembling a navy here for the attack on the Spanish. In 1820, Cochrane's navy stormed a fortress in Valdívia defended by over 700 men. The story is told in the Museo de Mar Almirante Cochrane, formerly the Scottish aristocrat's home.

Most of this enchanting city, however, is spread out over the hills that overlook the basin – there are 41 in all. Houses cling to the hillsides and many can be reached only by a network of funiculars which run almost vertically up from the port district.

Close to Valparaíso lies Viña del Mar, a seaside town, which is generally considered to be the prettiest in Chile. The town, which is on the edge of a forest, is built around wide, tree-lined boulevards which are served by *victorias* (horse-drawn carriages). It has scores of beautiful gardens, as well as some of the most beautiful beaches on the Pacific coast. The president of Chile has his summer retreat here, as do thousands of well-to-do Chileans and Argentinians who throng the beaches and help push up prices. Viña is the venue for all sorts of cultural events, including an annual song festival and regular rodeos.

Imagine the *huasos* dressed in their finest, while under a pergola girls serve out wine or *chicha* maize beer, and spicy *empanada* snacks. Guitarists accompany a country singer as the *cueca* dancing begins. Strutting like a rooster in his spurred boots, the *huaso* chooses his partner for the *cueca de punto y taco*, a dance that begins with loud stamping but ends with the once-reluctant cowgirl wrapped in an ardent embrace. Another couple may be dancing the *cueca refalosa*, whose movements suggest the couple are sliding on mud. Then a bottle is placed on the dance floor for the *costillar*; the couple who succeed in executing the intricate steps without knocking the bottle over win the show. In the rodeo itself, bullfighters win points for

every *atajada* in which they prevent the young bulls from running the length of the arena.

The Central Valley reaches southwards past Santiago to the Bío-Bío river, providing magnificent vistas of both the snow-capped Andes and the fertile orchards and vineyards beneath. If you are prevented from seeing the mountains from the capital due to the increasing problem of smog and pollution, then it is less than half an hour's drive from downtown Santiago to the Andes themselves. There are towns and villages here, but instead of picturesque Indian communities, you will find only modern ones which rely on skiing and thermal springs. While the skiing in resorts such as Portillo and Farellones is excellent, it has little to do with the real Chile or its culture.

About 30 miles south-west of Santiago lies the village of Pomaire, renowned throughout the country and beyond for its ceramics. Famous, too, are its succulent pork dishes. Naïve pottery animals are produced by the craftsmen of this small town to designs that have been handed down from generation to

This Chilota, an inhabitant of the island of Chiloé, holds up a string of cholgas (*small dried mussels*). *Fishing is the main industry of the island and it is hardly surprising that it abounds with legends of the sea.*

generation; they are much sought after by collectors of folk art. At Colchagua, slender poplars shade typical *huaso* houses with their tiled canopies. Here, craftsmen produce beautiful baskets from wheat straw.

Much of the Central Valley is reminiscent of the Mediterranean, with intensive cultivation of fruit, vines and livestock. But the region is by no means as tranquil as it looks today: this is the region of the great estates that Allende's Socialist government tried to break up, provoking political ferment. And in 1985 the area was hit by a catastrophic earthquake, which ensured that few Chileans forget that the Andes are still very much in formation. It is in this heartland – the most beautiful and fertile region – that two-thirds of Chile's population lives, and where the bulk of the country's industrial activity goes on.

Talca is the most important industrial city in the south of the central region. Located in the heart of vineyards, wheat and cattle land, this is still very much *huaso* country. It was here that the agreement for the independence of Chile was signed, in 1818. Chile's liberation memorabilia are housed in the Museo O'Higginiano, where the country's liberator grew up. Just south of Talca lies Chillán, where Bernardo O'Higgins was actually born.

Rocked by quakes

The Chilean capital, Santiago, lies 60 miles east of the Pacific. The city, which houses some 4 million people, was founded in 1541 by Don Pedro de Valdivia, but since then it has been destroyed three times – twice by the Indians and once, in 1674, by a massive earthquake. The 16th-century church of San Francisco is one of the few buildings of any note that have survived since the city's foundation. Though much of its architectural charm has long been swept away, the city has wonderful parks; much of its planning was carried out by Vicuña Mackenna, a politician and artist who created a central grid around the Plaza de Armas.

In the heart of downtown Santiago stands Santa Lucia Hill. It was on this spot that Valdivia founded the city, and it was from here that the last Spanish governor defended it against attacks by independence-seeking *Chilenos*. Vicuña Mackenna carried out O'Higgins' plan to transform the hill into the beautiful park which is today one of Santiago's great tourist attractions. Cerro San Cristóbal, near the Plaza Italia, stands 1200 feet high and is crowned by a massive statue of the Virgin Mary, a gift to Chile from the French government. There is a cable car from the city centre, which runs every 14 seconds and takes passengers up more than 3000 feet to a terrace close to the summit. Here there are gardens, paths and cafés where Santiagans and visitors can while away a couple of hours enjoying the

This paisano *is wearing a dark poncho, typical of the south. His horse is everything to him: his living, his means of transport and his companion.*

stunning panorama, away from the roar of streets choked by trucks and *colectivos* (small buses).

At night, the figure is floodlit and seems to float high above the city, while the bars and restaurants of the Bellavista district below provide more bohemian comforts. La Moneda, the presidential palace built by the Spanish in 1799 as a national treasure-house, bears no scars from Pinochet's bombing and soldiers can still be seen changing the guard here.

Springs, lakes and waterfalls

The city of Concepción and the Bío-Bío river mark the beginning of Chile's most stunning region, where volcanoes, lakes and forests are preserved in national parks besieged by tourists from Santiago during the summer months. These visitors provide subsistence for the Mapuche Indians, who controlled the area until 1881

The forests of the south are exploited for timber. These giant conifers with names such as coihues, ñires *and* lengues *have no equivalent elsewhere in the world.*

but now make a living from their handicrafts. This is a land of rain, rivers, volcanic hot springs, lakes, spectacular waterfalls and endless forests. Villarica is without question one of the most beautiful of Chile's scores of lakes. The town of Pucón has boomed in recent years as a holiday spot. It first became famous when Britain's Queen Elizabeth II stayed here during her state visit to Chile in 1968, and it has remained popular because of the beauty of the surrounding countryside. The massive Mount Villarica, a 10,000-foot volcano, looms over a nearby lake. Its huge, permanently snow-clad crater, which last erupted in 1985, gives off a constant stream of white smoke and lava particles. Species that are unique to the region grow here, notably the *araucaria*, which is a primitive type of pine tree, somewhat like the monkey-puzzle.

The region's many visitors have plenty of other lakes to choose from: Puyehue, Llanquihue, Rupanco and the Lago Todos los Santos (Lake of All Saints). Osorno is the main road and rail hub for the district, while a pass also leads into nearby Argentina. The Puyehue National Park offers sweeping views of the region's volcanoes. Llanquihue, the third largest lake in South America, is overlooked by the twin volcanoes of Osorno and Calbuco. The former attracts experienced climbers, and a ski club operates there too. The most beautiful of Chile's lakes, set within the Vicente Pérez National Park and right next to the Argentinian border, is the Lago Todos los Santos. From Peulla or Petrohué it is possible to travel into Argentina towards Bariloche, though many visitors are content to take a tourist boat to the island of Margarita on the middle of the lake.

This is the heartland of the Araucans. Cut off for

This is the araucaria, *the tree of the Araucan Indians. It can grow to a height of 160 feet and bears an edible fruit similar to the almond.*

Opposite: On her breast, this Araucan women wears a silver trapelacuha, *and around her head a ribbon – the* trarilonco *– from which another piece of jewellery is sometimes suspended.*

Temuco is the Araucan capital, where the Indians come to market to sell sheep, ponchos and craft items.

centuries from contact with the Spanish and their European successors, the Araucans still maintain important aspects of their culture. In the village of Ruca Ruqui, for example, a visitor might find Indian women weaving ponchos decorated with geometric designs. On a festival day, these women might put on their traditional silver *trapelacuha*, magnificent pendants covering the whole chest. On their heads they wear the *trarilonco*, a turban or headscarf from which hang silver adornments. This finery can be seen at the *nguillatún,* or annual festival, led by a sorceress.

The coastal city of Concepción is now Chile's third largest, and an industrial centre dominated by coal-mines, textiles, agricultural processing, petrochemicals and a massive steel works. The setting is beautiful: the city is not. Yet the harsh wet climate has made it more

palatable to German migrants than those more used to the sun. One of its few points of genuine interest is La Planchada Fort, which defended Concepción for two centuries from attacks by the Araucans, and today is maintained as a landmark by the city.

Southern extremes

The Pan-American Highway terminates at Puerto Montt, on the northern edge of the Gulf of Ancud. To the south, Chile is a network of fjords, lakes and canals, and fishing takes over from agriculture as the main source of income. Puerto Montt, with its wooden houses and brightly coloured tiled roofs, was founded in 1852 by a group of German immigrants, whose descendants still live there. The harbour is a mass of little fishing boats, many of which belong to the Chilotas, the inhabitants of the islands of the Chilean archipelago. These boats bring merchandise for sale in the town: on board, fishermen can be seen cutting open the *picoroco,* (a shellfish) which is eaten alive with lemon juice.

Chiloé is one of South America's largest coastal islands. It is wet and foggy like the mainland, and covered with lakes and conifer forest. The island is 155 miles long and is reached by ferry from the mainland. It also has wonderful scenery, although the climate is harsh. Despite their remoteness, these islands were settled very early. The original inhabitants were the Chonos Indians, but they were displaced with the arrival of the Europeans and, with them, the Mapuche Indians.

There is a 16th-century wooden church at Achao which shows the influence of the Jesuits, while other churches were built by the Franciscans who succeeded them. The capital, Castro, was founded in 1567 by Martín Ruiz de Gamboa as a safe haven for Spanish ships sailing through the channels of the archipelago. Later, during the wars of independence, Chile's last Spanish governor took advantage of this safe haven when he fled here from the rebels – even going so far as to offer the island to the British, who turned his offer down. Today, large areas are still covered with pine forest, though the relatively temperate climate and rich soil does support agriculture, sustaining a population of over 100,000.

Despite Chiloé's harshness, it is perhaps one of the liveliest places in Chile, and most of the country's dances – *zamba, refalosa, costillar* and *cueca chilota* – come from there. Moreover, it is a place of myths and legends. Many of these are thought to have originated with the Chonos Indians, but over the centuries, they have been adopted by all Chileans. The island fishermen firmly believe in the sea fairy, *la Pincoya,* who takes possession of men's minds and drags them to the bottom of the sea. They also believe in *el Tranco,* the spirit with penetrating eyes who seduces young girls; and in *el Calenche*, a phantom ship, which sails through the coastal waters at night, manned by a crew of maimed people who sing in sepulchral voices.

Chilean Patagonia and Tierra del Fuego have some of the wildest and most stunning landscapes on earth. Less than 3 per cent of Chile's population live among the icebergs, fjords, lakes, lagoons, ice fields and gigantic

mountains that comprise almost one-third of the country's land mass. It rains constantly, plant life is all but non-existent, and the few trees that manage to survive the conditions are twisted into tortured shapes by icy winds which blow up to 100 miles per hour. Yet there are animals which do survive, including llamas, pumas and foxes.

In the Torres del Paine National Park are condors, flamingoes, ostrich-like rheas and black-necked swans. This superb park is set in the Torres del Paine Cordillera, whose highest peak reaches 7875 feet, and you can travel to it from Puerto Natales some 80 miles away. The trekking here is as good as anywhere in the world: camping in specially built refuges, visitors journey through a wilderness where they are unlikely to see other signs of human life. The three towers of granite after which the park is named rise dramatically from a windy plain where the wildlife includes Chilean deer, guanaco (wild llama), and countless predators including puma. The Lago de Grey and its glacier can be visited by boat, from which you can also see bergs calving into the water. Close to Puerto Natales is the Cueva Milodón, where in 1895 a Swedish explorer found the remains of a gigantic sloth. Other caves contain signs of one of the earliest human habitations. Bordering the Argentinian frontier and the Torres del Paine is the Parque Nacional O'Higgins, which contains two spectacular glaciers, Balmaceda and Serrano. Views of these glaciers sliding into the water can be had from the steamer that makes a daily trip close to them in the summer months.

Tierra del Fuego, a windswept landmass suitable only for sheep grazing – and in many areas not even that – is largely made up of Isla Grande, which is divided between Chile and Argentina. Puerto Williams, on the southernmost island of Navarino across the Beagle Channel, is an extraordinary sight. The world's most southerly habitation is just a scrap in a massive landscape, from which pilot boats come out to escort ships along the winding Beagle Channel. Fur seals, penguins and other fauna give visitors a foretaste of sights awaiting the lucky few able to travel southwards from here to the Antarctic continent.

It was to Tierra del Fuego, not far from Puerto Williams, that the young British scientist Charles Darwin came aboard the *Beagle* on a naval hydrographic mission in 1834. During Darwin's visit, the Indians of Tierra del Fuego came calling and, attracted by the prospect of clothes, tools and instruments, had to be frightened away by gunshot. 'It was almost ludicrous to watch through a glass the Indians, as often as the shot struck the water, take up stones and as a bold defence, throw them towards the ship,' wrote Darwin. Today none of these 'Fuegians' of the Yaganes people survive.

Punta Arenas is the second most southerly city in the world after Ushuaia in Argentina. Despite its extreme latitude, Punta Arenas has been an important port since it was first settled by the Spanish in 1584. It is strategically placed on the northern shore of the Strait of Magellan which, before the construction of the Panama Canal, was the only route from the Pacific to the Atlantic to avoid the treacherous Cape Horn. The fortunes of Punta Arenas have recently been boosted by the discovery of oil and natural gas deposits in the region. Cape Horn is the steep headland on Horn Island, in southernmost Chile. This is the last landmass before the vast white wilderness of Antarctica and the tip of the world.

The days of the vast estate, with its colonial-style hacienda, *are probably numbered in Chile, as they are throughout Latin America.*

Ecuador

Giant volcanic peaks loom over the central highlands of the
smallest of the Andean republics. Modern Ecuador formed the
northern fastnesses of the Inca empire – today, it is one of the
region's most stable countries. Its mountains and jungles are also
home to several Indian peoples, most of whom have succeeded in
the hard task of adapting to new conditions, while retaining their
traditional crafts and customs. Off Ecuador's coast, meanwhile,
lies the wildlife paradise of the Galapagos Islands – inspiration to
Charles Darwin in his work on the theory of evolution.

In the 'Valley of Volcanoes', a peasant from Cotopaxi looks over the Quilotca lagoon, relieved no doubt that the status of the huasipongo – *the serf attached for life to his landlord – has been abolished.*

Previous page: *The heart of the agave contains a sap which is used to make* pulque, *a strangely flavoured Ecuadorian drink. The leaves are well protected so, in order to get to the heart, this woman from the Pichincha region has first to strip off the serrated edges.*

Thousands of iguanas, those astonishing antediluvian survivors, live on the Galapagos Islands today. Despite its awesome appearance, however, this five-foot saurian is a herbivore.

The Incas' Northern Realm

Instead of shocking visitors with the human conflict that plagues its larger neighbours, Ecuador amazes people with its natural wonders. They range from the world's highest active volcano, through the Amazon jungles of Oriente, to the offshore Galapagos Islands whose unique animal and plant life provided some of the first clues to the origin of the species.

Small is beautiful

The smallest and most tranquil of the Andean countries, Ecuador is more diverse in climate than you might expect from a country situated on the Equator. Its capital, Quito, has a fresh, spring-like air, because of its elevation, 9350 feet above sea level, and the surrounding snow-dusted volcanoes. The country's small size means that visitors can explore the Amazon without suffering interminable days on river-boats, see Inca relics without travelling the length and breadth of the Andes, and enjoy numerous Pacific beaches and Spanish colonial towns with ease.

Ecuador is divided into three culturally and politically distinct regions: the tropical coastal plain, with its fertile alluvial soil; the Andes; and the Amazon jungle, to the east of the *cordillera,* which had been spared the massive deforestation carried out elsewhere, until the recent discovery of oil.

Today, Ecuador's rain forest is under serious threat, and perhaps its greatest conservation hope is a boundary dispute with Peru. This is a hangover from the days of Simón Bolívar's Gran Colombia, from which a much larger Ecuador was carved in 1830. But neighbouring Peru gradually nibbled away at its upper Amazon territories until the 1940s, when full-scale war erupted and Quito was forced to cede. Today, Ecuadorian maps proudly but unrealistically show the country to be much larger than is internationally accepted.

From the north of the country to the south, the Andes divide the coastal plain from the Amazon jungle. About two-fifths of the population still live in the mountains, but there is a steady move towards the coastal region and the promise of a better life. The mountain Indians, however, have not migrated. They prefer to stay in their traditional lands, scratching a living as peasant farmers or as *peones* on huge coffee and cocoa plantations.

Much of Ecuador's upland landscape is dominated by the greatest concentration of volcanoes in the world – topped by Cotopaxi, the 19,350-foot cone that last erupted in 1928, but which continuously emits clouds of steam from its lava-filled crater. Despite some localised spots where fertile volcanic soils support a dense population, the upland *páramo* is a bleak region.

Mixing of the nations

Of the South American nations, it is Ecuador whose society remains most intact, though new oil wealth is fast eradicating links with the past. About 40 per cent of Ecuador's population is *mestizo* (mixed race) and another 40 per cent is Indian; the rest is made up of Europeans and those of African origin whose ancestors were brought to work in the plantations. Though Ecuador has one of the continent's smallest populations, it is the most densely populated.

Ecuador was once part of the Inca empire, but archaeological relics show that long before then tribes inhabited the central coastal region. Stone Age tools from 9000 BC have been found, while in the centuries preceding the Inca conquest, two distinct cultures had emerged – the Caras from the lowlands and the Quitus

The Costa, Ecuador's Pacific coast, was one enormous banana plantation until the 1960s when the market collapsed. Ecuador still exports large quantities of the fruit, but now derives most of its wealth from oil.

People and birds share the shrimp and lobsters on the shore of Ancorcito, in the state of Guayos. Here, warm currents mix with the icy waters of the Pacific.

The Saraguro Indians defy the passage of time. In the past they have defended their identity against the Inca conquerors. Nowadays they are famous for their longevity; in Loja it is not unusual to live for 100 years.

Among the Indians of Ecuador, the Otavalo reigns supreme. This water-bearer, with his immaculate white trousers, poncho, black plait and felt hat, is the representative of a people proud of its success. The Otavalos are not only skilled craftsmen; they are also shrewd businessmen.

from the mountains. Two other peoples, the Cañari and the Puruhás, completed the alliance of Ecuadorian peoples who fiercely resisted the northward advance of Topa Inca as he subjected this new territory during the second half of the 15th century.

The conquest of Ecuador by his successor Huayna Capac represented the greatest expansion of the Inca empire. On Huayna Capac's death in 1526 the empire was divided between two stepbrothers, always a sure recipe for war. Atahualpa emerged victorious over his rival Huascar in 1532, just in time to succumb to the *conquistador* Francisco Pizarro.

The Inca heritage stretches beyond the use of the traditional Andean language, Quechua; the rich indigenous culture includes numerous festivals during which the deity being honoured is only nominally Christian. An Indian fiesta such as the harvest festival – celebrated on Corpus Christi – is an excuse for processions, drinking and dancing.

Cuenca in the south is the most vibrant centre for Ecuadorian crafts and folklore; traditions here have survived because of the city's isolated position and because of the successful mix of races and cultures over the centuries. The Incas originally formed a settlement at Cuenca, then the Spanish came and, impressed by the temperate climate and the skills of the Indians, established large craft workshops. Their successors have survived to this day and are largely responsible for the town's prosperity. They are hat-makers, wickerwork artisans, potters, goldsmiths, alabaster cutters and wood-carvers.

But crafts are not the only traditions to flourish. Most impressive is the Indian overlay to Catholic fiestas. Indians and *montuvios* (the name given to Ecuador's often mixed-race rural population) alike take great pride in contributing to a festival's costs and in assuming communal duties and responsibilities. Despite the financial burden they impose on a community, festivals bond local people and redistribute wealth – for many, festival-time is the only chance to eat meat.

The northern Andes constitute the most densely populated rural area in Ecuador. In pre-Columbian times, the fertile soil fostered the growth of large settled societies, which were ultimately united under the Inca empire. Spanish colonisation was disastrous, however. The Indians were forced into serfdom on the *haciendas* (estates) and there they remained as slaves until the status of the *huasipongos* was abolished.

Huasipongos were Indians and their families who were bought and sold as part and parcel of a *hacienda*. They were obliged to work for nothing but the right to farm their own tiny plots of land. Since these captive labourers have been set free, the owners of the old *haciendas* have broken up their estates, keeping the best land for themselves and converting it to livestock farming which requires minimal manpower. Many of the former *huasipongos* have been forced to move from the region and to scratch a living on the mountainsides with the other Indians, or to migrate to the coastal plain. A few have found employment in the mountains or as labourers on the building sites of Quito, Cuenca or one of the other Andean towns.

The liberation of the *huasipongos* has encouraged more cultural cross-fertilisation in the Ecuadorian

This shepherdess, whip and lasso in hand, comes from hardy stock. Her language, however, is surprisingly gentle and full of coy diminutives, such as señorcito *(little sir) rather than* señor.

Andes: a process which was already more advanced here than in most Latin American countries. The cost of this has been a dilution of ancient traditions. Although Quechua is still spoken and Inca ancestry is still a source of pride, there has been a move towards using Spanish as well as Quechua and away from traditional costume, although brightly coloured ponchos and the extraordinary hats of the Otavalo people are still worn. There has also been a decline in some of the traditional celebrations. Nevertheless, some groups – notably the Saraguros from Loja, the Salasacas from between Ambato and Baños, and the Otavalos from north of Quito – continue to cling stubbornly to the old ways, just as they did in the face of the invading Incas and, later, the Spanish *conquistadores*.

Mestizos, traditional tribespeople and representatives of modern Ecuador all gather at the huge markets which take over most Andean towns once a week. Each town has its own market day, with the result that traders work them in rotation.

Quito: heritage of mankind

Quito, the capital of Ecuador, is a place of stunning beauty. Situated 9350 feet above sea level in a long, narrow valley at the foot of the slumbering volcano, Pichincha, it is surrounded by lush green fields and snow-capped peaks. It is only 15 miles south of the Equator but its altitude guarantees a mild, spring-like climate all year round. The old city with its red-tiled houses and colonial structures retains much 16th-century Spanish architecture and has 86 churches. Yet for all this, it is not Ecuador's largest city – a distinction reserved for Guayaquil.

The city was named after the Quitu Indians who arrived here before the 11th century. In 1487 it became the northern capital of the Inca empire and in 1536 it was taken for the Spanish crown by Sebastián de Benalcázar. Despite the fact that all traces of the pre-Inca and Inca civilisation have vanished, Quito is a city of great historical interest. It was not, ironically, the Spanish who destroyed the city's pre-Columbian heritage but the Incas themselves. Rather than let their temples be desecrated by the colonists, the Incas under their general, Rumiñahui, laid waste to their treasures in 1534. As a result there are almost no Inca ruins.

The Spanish left more tangible marks on the city. Quito was once the administrative and religious centre for the whole of the northern Andes, when the government of all Spanish dominions was administered from Lima. In 1978, UNESCO declared the city part of mankind's cultural heritage, because of the splendour of its colonial architecture, and the paintings and sculpture which decorate its churches. The old town is a living museum and no modern development is permitted, but artistic and intellectual innovation thrive. Quito has a brilliant academic and artistic life, and the old colonial town has been successfully and tastefully extended into a modern city, which begins beyond the Parque el Ejido.

Since Ecuadorian independence was won, at the Battle of Pichincha in 1822, Quito has been saddled with Ecuador's massive and ungainly bureaucratic establishment. It is a colourful city, but even the rituals and ceremonies are conducted with an air of solemnity untypical of Latin America.

Not all the inhabitants follow Quito's less than effervescent code of conduct. New arrivals from the surrounding Andean villages – mainly craftsmen and their families – crowd into one-room garrets in the old colonial buildings, now abandoned by the upper classes in favour of modern apartment blocks. This new culture has its own customs brought from the villages. Their festivals and marriages are more lively and spirited than those of the city's established middle classes, and act as a welcome light relief from the pervading atmosphere of seriousness. Other communities from the mountains also migrate temporarily into the capital. Men seek

Opposite: Adobe walls and a crude thatched roof protect the single room where an entire family eats and sleeps. The fertile land of the region is owned by a handful of wealthy landlords; as a result, former huasipongos are forced to farm the poorer, eroded soil of the mountain slopes.

Such is the age-old simplicity of her life that this Saraguro woman from the Loja region can almost be imagined as a biblical character.

seasonal work on the building sites and their young women offer themselves as domestic servants. At the end of their stay, they return to their villages.

A tour of Quito's old quarter is complicated by numerous pickpockets. If the best-known street, La Ronda, proves too dangerous, the solution is to dive into the many churches along the way. Work began on the San Francisco church immediately after the city's foundation in 1534 (making it probably the first religious building the Spanish constructed in South America) and, though rebuilt after earthquake damage several times, it remains the finest, and largest, church in the capital. An adjoining museum shows Franciscan art dating back to the 16th century. For sheer opulence, meanwhile, nothing can beat the Jesuit church of La Compañía, richly adorned with several tons of gold, and including among its treasures a sumptuous painting of the the Virgen Dolorosa richly framed with gold and emeralds. In contrast, the city's Gothic-style cathedral on the Plaza de la Independencia is a stark structure.

No Latin American capital is complete without a building where the country's independence was formally proclaimed, and Quito's is the 17th-century church of San Agustín where Ecuador's founding fathers declared their sovereignty on August 10, 1809 – still celebrated annually as Independence Day.

Of Quito's museums, the best for pre-Columbian relics are the two musems that form the Museos de Banco Central – the Museo Arqueológica and the Museo Colonial y de Arte Religioso – while the Casa de Sucre shows life as it was lived in the colony and during the independence struggle. Antonio José de Sucre, who afterwards gave his name to Ecuador's national currency, was one of Simón Bolívar's top military commanders and it was he who defeated pro-Spanish royalists at Quito on May 21, 1822.

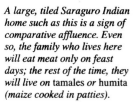

A large, tiled Saraguro Indian home such as this is a sign of comparative affluence. Even so, the family who lives here will eat meat only on feast days; the rest of the time, they will live on tamales *or* humita *(maize cooked in patties).*

Men with pigtails, women in shawls

The valleys of Ibarra and the lake region north of the capital are lush and green, and much of the land is given over to dairy farming – Cayambe is the Ecuadorian cheese capital. Even the desert valley of Chota, which cuts across the northern Andes after Ibarra, is productive, with large sugar-cane plantations, worked by the descendants of African slaves.

Northern Ecuador is also famous for its population of Otavalo Indians, who are centred around the town bearing their name on the shore of Lake San Pablo. They have retained many of the traditions of their ancestors, in particular, their dress. Otavalo men wear pigtails, felt hats and blue ponchos; the women use gaudier shawls, coloured headcloths and embroidered bodices. As dedicated farmers, they are immensely attached to the land, but they have also developed their crafts to compensate for the poverty of the Andean soil. They have developed a sales and distribution system for their wares, which have proved irresistible to foreign travellers. Today, their wares can be found displayed, not only along the roadsides and in the markets of Ecuador, but also in the fashionable boutiques of New York and London.

Overshadowed by two volcanoes, the town of Otavalo and its Saturday markets – specialising in woollen goods – draw huge crowds. The Otavalos are shrewd businessmen with a highly developed sense of their responsibilities towards one another. The profits from their commercial endeavours are ploughed back, financing festivals and other community projects. In this way, the Otavalos have managed to strike that uneasy balance between preserving their identity and adapting to the realities of the modern world.

Near Ecuador's northern frontier with Colombia is Esmeraldas, on the Pacific coast. This is home to the Cayapas Indians, descended from slaves who won their freedom from the region's sugar plantations. Today, they live in wooden shacks on the banks of the Esmeraldas river. In the 1950s and 1960s, Esmeraldas enjoyed a brief period of prosperity from its banana crops, but this lasted only as long as the boom in banana prices, brought on by a drop in harvests in Central America. Since then, the *haciendas* have gradually converted to the production of palm oil, but even this is secondary to the region's two new sources of prosperity – oil, which is piped from the Amazon for refining, and tourism.

It is wash day in the San Pedro lake. The local Indians pound the clothes between rocks or tread them underfoot, using the sap from plant stems as a form of soap.

These ragged princesses of the Saraguro people might live a subsistence existence, but their jewellery is a reminder of a brilliant past.

*The nimble fingers of an
Indian girl who has learnt to
spin in early childhood will
soon transform this ball of
sheep's wool into a fine
single thread.*

Esmeraldas itself is a town of contrasts and contradictions, with an old, rather charmless colonial quarter, a black ghetto, a beach area with a proliferation of gaudy stuccoed holiday homes, and Balao with modern petro-chemical installations. In many ways, the contrasting character of Esmeraldas is a microcosm of Ecuador as a whole.

The area around Esmeraldas was once forested, but this has long since vanished. The coastal road which leads south from Esmeraldas towards Santo Domingo de los Colorados is flanked by abandoned banana plantations. Here and there, these have been replaced by splendid, new palm-oil plantations, each dominated by an imposing colonial-style home set in the middle of manicured lawns with a group of workers' huts perched on stilts nearby.

Volcanic paradise

The Cotopaxi National Park lies south of the capital. Here, hikers walk in the shadow of the 19,350-foot Cotopaxi, the highest active volcano in the world. Thrusting volcanic activity has raised this section of the Andean *cordillera* and produced the gigantic, snow-covered craters which form Ecuador's 'valley of the volcanoes'. The most spectacular view of the peaks, jutting from the cloudbase, is from the summit of Cotopaxi itself – but reaching that involves a tough 10-hour climb, starting in the early hours of the morning and suitable only for experienced mountaineers. Nine of the peaks can also be seen – in more comfort – from Latacunga, a town some 85 miles from the capital which has twice been destroyed by the volcano. Hiking beside turquoise lakes, or visiting Indian markets where women still wear the distinctive pork-pie hat, are the chief attractions here.

Baños is named after the hot springs which were once popular. Despite the declining fortune of the springs themselves, many of the small hotels and tourist shops that sprang up to serve the visitors have survived. Baños also has a brightly coloured church, typical of many found throughout the Andes, with walls of sky blue, pistachio green, brown or yellow. Overlooked by the 16,400-foot summit of Volcán Tungurahua, Baños is also the site of a traditional pilgrimage held each October to honour the Virgen de Agua Santa (Virgin of Holy Water), who is thought to be responsible for several miracles. The basilica in the centre of the town has a series of paintings depicting many of the miracles attributed to her.

Ríobamba, the most southerly town in the 'valley of the volcanoes', is more modern in feel. All traces of its pre-Columbian heritage were erased by the Spanish centuries ago, and many of its fine colonial buildings, in turn, fell victim to the great earthquake of 1797. None the less, this city, situated 9800 feet above sea level, is one of Ecuador's most typically Andean – indeed, it boasts the nickname 'Sultan of the Andes'. As well as the opportunities to climb a number of nearby volcanic peaks, Ríobamba also offers a Saturday market that is a serious rival to Otavalo's – with fine arrays of woven belts (*fajas*), shawls, blanket pins (*tupus*) and embroidered dresses – and has an interesting museum of religious artefacts.

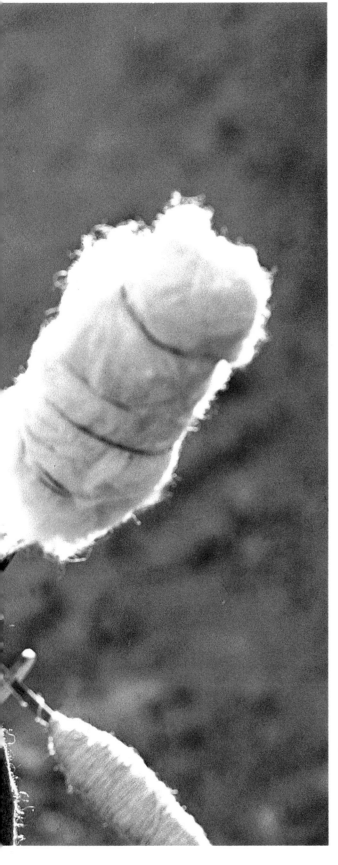

A shepherdess herds her landlord's flock near the town of Latacunga, in a region chilled by icy winds from the Cotopaxi volcano.

The carludovica humilis grows only in the coastal region or in the Equatorial Amazon. It is a close relative of the palm tree from which paja toquilla is extracted for the manufacture of Ecuador's well-known, but misnamed, 'Panama' hats.

The true Panama hat does not come from Panama but from Ecuador. The name came about because, in the past, they were generally exported through Panama. Making a quality hat is a long and skilled process, and the very best can fetch several hundred dollars.

Harbour lights in the south

Guayaquil is Ecuador's largest city, with a population of around 1.7 million. It lies on the heavily wooded banks of the chocolate-coloured Guayas river, some 12 miles from the Gulf of Guayaquil. The river is navigable by the largest of ocean vessels, which makes this natural estuary one of the Pacific's most important ports.

Despite its size, economic pre-eminence and its ancient beginnings, in 1537, Guayaquil has never managed to wrest administrative control of the country from Quito. There is an intense rivalry between the two cities, but the desire of the people of Guayaquil for the capital to be moved to their own city is not merely a matter of vanity or civic pride – it stems from a deep-seated belief that Ecuador cannot be governed effectively from a remote Andean city, notoriously reluctant to adapt to the economic and technological demands of a modern economy. Nevertheless, Ecuador may be equally difficult to govern from a stifling coastal city that sprawls over mangrove swamps infested, until recently, with malaria.

Malecón Simón Bolívar, the main riverside boulevard, retains some of Guayaquil's early charm. At its northern end is the oldest part of the city, Las Peñas, a picturesque maze of cobbled streets and alleys overlooked by dilapidated wooden houses.

There have been times when Guayaquil has come close to winning supremacy over Quito. At the beginning of the 19th century, when the country gained independence, there was talk of the coastal region becoming an autonomous republic, but this came to nothing. Guayaquil's failure to achieve real status probably lies in the fact that, despite its commercial supremacy, it lacks the innate authority of a capital. Two disastrous fires in, 1896 and 1902, destroyed many of the wooden structures on which its fame might have rested.

The city has none of the music or the dancing which are so much part of the magic of Latin America. Its hard-headed masters and the surrounding plantations have failed to create a tropical coastal culture, or to encourage the city to compete with Quito as a centre of excellence in education and the arts. For all that, it does have a few noteworthy buildings, including the church

The true Ecuadorian 'Panama' is supple, washable and perfectly waterproof. This labourer is employed in a Cuenca workshop which is internationally renowned for the quality of its hats.

A weaver works at his loom in the streets of Chinlonga. Ponchos are produced in different colours according to the customer's origins.

of Santo Domingo, dating from 1548, not to mention a huge cemetery, filled with the sumptuous tombs of the wealthy dead, each one of which is in itself a minor, if fantastical and often grotesque, work of art.

Guayaquil lacks identity. As a result, the tens of thousands of *montuvios* (mountain people) who have flocked here from the Andes are essentially displaced persons. In the poorer quarters of the city, workers swelter in tiny, unventilated one-room concrete apartments. On the other hand, the affluent citizens of Guayaquil have set up summer residences in beach resorts such as Salinas and Playas. They now far out-

number the local fisherfolk, and their luxurious holiday apartment blocks and casinos dwarf the older buildings.

Machala, south of the city, is sometimes called the 'banana capital of the world'. Indeed, there is little to do here except unzip these fruits at the international banana festival, held in September. Offshore, in the gulf,

however, the island of Jambelí is a more attractive spot – a jungle of weirdly twisted mangroves with long sandy beaches on its far side. It is easily reached from Puerto Bolívar on the coast, close to Ecuador's border with Peru.

Cuenca and the secrets of a long life

In Inca and earlier times, the whole of southern Ecuador was heavily populated, as ruins such as those at Ingapirca north of Cuenca testify. Today, however, the Loja region is inhabited mainly by the descendants of European colonists rather than by Indians. These peasant farmers scratch a simple living from sugar-cane at comparatively modest altitudes of around 6000 feet above sea level. The soil and climate are ideal for growing such crops, but the steepness of the land and the lack of any adequate roads across it make large-scale farming all but impossible.

Life is hard but healthy for the inhabitants. People are generally long-lived; it is not uncommon to live to 100, and there are several well-documented cases of people living to 130 and 140 years old, a phenomenon that has interested both anthropologists and medical researchers.

Opposite: These bristly black pigs in Chinlonga market, will soon be turned into succulent hornados (*grilled pork*), *which is sold in the street, accompanied by* canelitas, *an infusion of cinnamon and sugar-cane in alcohol.*

The market in Otavalo is famous all over Ecuador. These Indian women, in their embroidered blouses and heavy gold jewellery, are selling cabuya (*rope-soled sandals); women's sandals are blue and men's are white. All Otavalo women cover their heads with the* fachalina, *a square of dark cotton.*

Despite extensive research, however, no one has been able to explain just why southern Ecuador fosters such longevity.

Cuenca, the jewel of the southern Ecuadorian Andes, is the country's third largest city. It has long been isolated in the stunningly beautiful, mountain-rimmed Pucarabamba valley and has been relatively untouched by commerce or tourism. Its charm lies in the preservation of its colonial style. Lying beside the Pan-American Highway at 8517 feet above sea level,

Cuenca is a centre for the manufacture of leather goods and Panama hats – made from the fan-shaped leaves of the palm-like jipijapa plant, itself named after the lowland town of Jipijapa. It is also one of the few cities in the world to boast two cathedrals, of which the more modern one (started in 1885) houses a famous crowned Virgin. It also has some exceptionally fine modern stained-glass windows, creating wonderful effects of light and dark inside the cathedral.

Established in 1557 on the site of a major Inca town, Cuenca is reminiscent of Peru's Cuzco in that, here and there, fragments of Inca stonework underpin colonial buildings. The city also hosts some of Ecuador's most colourful Christmas festivities, notably the spectacular Pasada del Niño Viajero (Parade of the Travelling Child), held on Christmas Eve each year. People from the surrounding towns and villages pour into the city in trucks or battered cars or on donkeys or horseback, all festooned with various symbols of abundance – from bunches of bananas or clusters of pepper to wads of dollar notes. Children dress up in their traditional costumes or as figures from the Bible and march through the streets to the sound of guitars and the thin, eerie whistle of the *rondador*, the small Ecuadorian panpipe. A week later, on New Year's Eve, there are more parades, and effigies (often caricatures of prominent politicians) are burnt on bonfires, to symbolise the passing of the old year.

Although Ecuador's Inca ruins do not bear comparison to Peru's, a visit to Pumapungo is worth while: this was the birthplace of the last undisputed Inca emperor, Huayna Capac. Farther north is the Inca fortress of Ingapirca, where excavation work is still in progress in the hope of finding relics to match those of Cuzco.

Cuenca is situated in the narrowest stretch of the

Their deadly curare-*tipped arrows were not enough to protect the Aucas Indians from the colonial rubber barons.*

The Aucas have survived wave after wave of interlopers in their Amazon homeland, but today they risk becoming little more than tourist attractions.

The Colorado Indians are the very height of fashion. They cover the shaved portion of their heads and parts of their bodies with a red pigment called achiote.

Andes and is therefore not far, across the mountains, from the Amazon jungle. The nearest forest region, the Oriente, is home to one of the Amazon's best-known nations (the Jivaros) who were once renowned for their ferocity and for shrinking heads. Today, the Jivaros live a peaceful existence in the forest and the shrunken heads are faked for the tourists.

Nevertheless, the tribe is under attack from mainstream Ecuadorian society which, desperate for land, continues to chip away at their territory. The Jivaros continue to fight back, no longer with *curare*-tipped arrows, but with the white man's 'system'; they have recently won the right in the courts to be known by their traditional name, the Shuars. They have established a federation and work co-operatives, and have instigated a literacy campaign, which is broadcast by transistor radio to every village.

Into the Amazon jungle

Ecuador's Amazon province is – or was – its 'empty quarter', in which Indians were largely left alone to pursue their traditional lifestyle – until they were rudely

interrupted by cattle ranchers and oil workers. For all its former emptiness, however, this eastern portion of the Amazon valley comprises almost half the country's land area.

From Baños, a dirt road enters the Oriente. It winds east and then north through Tena and Baeza, before branching off to Quito in the west, or towards the oilfields of Coca and Lago Agrio in the east. In any direction, the going is hard but the journey gives a good picture of the Amazon today.

Life here is rooted in the past. The bitterness felt by the indigenous Amazon Indians towards white and mixed-race interlopers has not softened with time. From the mid-16th century to the late 19th century, the Oriente was the scene of running battles between whites and Indians which culminated in acts of horrific genocide by colonists hungry for rubber.

The commodity has changed, but the process goes on. The Auca Indians were for many Ecuadorians the very symbol of the Amazon peoples. Over the centuries, the nation was driven deeper and deeper into the jungle, eventually shunning all contact with the outside world. Nevertheless, the rubber barons managed to track them down and tried to press them into gathering rubber. They failed, and what was left of the Aucas returned to the depths of the jungle, swearing never again to consort with whites, *mestizos* or even other Indians. Oil prospectors then moved into the territory, and it took all the guile and courage of a small band of missionaries to avert an all-out bloodbath. It was one of the few

occasions in their history that missionaries tried to assume the characteristics of the society they were trying to convert. Instead of seeking to clothe the naked Aucas, they themselves undressed to show respect for the Indians' traditional values.

There are still a few Aucas left. One of the few things they have to show for centuries of persecution is the fact that they too have won the right to use their original name – the Huaoranis. Today, however, they are a shadow of their former proud selves – at times little more than a carnival sideshow acting out their lives for the benefit of tourists.

There are Amazonian peoples who have become even more integrated into the cultural hotchpotch of mixed-

The guana (*panpipes*) *lie at the heart of much Andean music, producing a haunting, eerie sound which seems to belong to another age.*

The beat of the bombo (*bass drum*) *alternates with that of the* tinya, *a small, two-sided drum made of llama skin. With a variety of flutes and stringed instruments, they constitute part of a typical Indian orchestra.*

race people that makes up the vast majority of the region's population. These include people who moved into the Oriente from the Andes and the descendants of the first mixing of Amazon Indians and Europeans. These people now lead a meagre existence, farming small plots cleared by slash-and-burn techniques, while hunting and fishing to supplement their diet.

Settlers only arrived in the Oriente in the wake of missionaries and traders, until the discovery of oil in 1972. Roads were built and small towns sprang up in the jungle. But the oil, like the rubber, will not last for ever. The main deposits in the Oriente are already nearing exhaustion and new finds are too sparse to sustain the boom of the last 20 years. The petrochemical

giants will soon move on to richer pastures, leaving the new Amazon population to struggle for survival. Such a rapid reversal in fortunes is nothing new in the Amazon. For centuries it has been on a roller-coaster of boom-and-bust and has yet to find a way of life that is sustainable: that will be achieved only by a change towards the traditional cultures of the Amazon and observance of the lessons of the jungle itself – giving generously, without taking excessively.

Access to the northern Oriente is through the town of Puyo, where travellers are courted by many of the 'jungle tour' operators they can expect to encounter heading eastwards. Macas, which lies southward at the edge of the *cordillera,* and Sucúa are located in territory

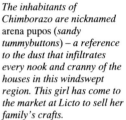

The inhabitants of Chimborazo are nicknamed arena pupos (sandy tummybuttons) *– a reference to the dust that infiltrates every nook and cranny of the houses in this windswept region. This girl has come to the market at Licto to sell her family's crafts.*

Although they observe the Christian calendar, Ecuadorian peasants have not forgotten their own traditional rites, some of which pre-date Inca times. In May and June in the sierra, *not a single week passes without some elaborate festival.*

that once belonged to the head-hunting Shuar Indians. Northwards from Puyo on the road to Coca lies the oil-country. Tena is the centre of much of the drilling activity, but it is also close to Misahuallí, a convenient place to view the jungle – though the forest here has been well trodden and much of the fauna is long gone. Farther down the Napo river lies the real rain forest, especially around the town of Coca (officially called Puerto Francisco de Orellana, after the 16th-century Spanish *conquistador* commander who left Pizarro's command and ended up floating all the way to Belém at the Amazon's mouth).

Declared an 'inheritance for humanity' by UNESCO, Quito is a jewel of colonial architecture. It has managed to make the transition to a modern capital without losing its character. Whole Andean communities set themselves up here on a temporary basis, eventually returning to their place of origin.

Footprints of evolution in the Galapagos Islands

'Nothing could be less inviting than the first appearance,' wrote the British naturalist Charles Darwin, recalling the moment he stepped ashore on the Galapagos Islands in 1835. Situated some 600 miles west of Ecuador, the 13 main volcanic islands and numerous islets contain many animals found nowhere else on earth. How, asked Darwin, would they have adapted themselves in such isolation?

Best known are the giant land tortoises that gave the islands their name, the flightless cormorants, and the marine iguanas. But it was a group of 14 finches, each of which had evolved into a distinct species, that fascinated Darwin. Seeing this diversity, Darwin – who had come to the islands on board the Royal Navy's HMS *Beagle*, bound on a round-the-world map-making expedition – realised that they must all have descended from a single ancestor.

The islands were claimed for Ecuador in 1831 by General José de Villamil and were later turned into a penal colony. The volcanic archipelago consists of five large islands and eight smaller ones, 42 islets and a scattering of rocks. Over the centuries, animals and plant seeds established themselves on the islands, carried there by the winds and ocean currents. Penguins and flamingoes, sea lions and iguanas, albatross and boobies comprise the unique combination of polar and tropical species.

The Galapagos were declared a national park by the government of Ecuador in 1959, and it is the wild life, together with the idyllic climate, which attracts tens of thousands of visitors every year and which justifies the Spanish name for the archipelago – *Encantadas,* the Enchanted Islands.

One of the most extraordinary characteristics of the animals on the Galapagos Islands was their lack of fear of people and their complete innocence in the face of predators. Darwin was fascinated that the animals slowly acquired defensive instincts after the first reported travellers to the islands began their indiscriminate slaughter.

That the islands have not changed more since then is a tribute to the Ecuadorean government's tourism policy, which thrives despite a disastrous fire on Isabela Island in 1985. Today, the islands constitute a large park with strict regulations for visitors. No one can tour the islands without an official guide and camping is tightly controlled. Access is limited to a number of special sites, which tourists visit by boat after arriving on Isla Baltra by air. Most of these tours are fixed in advance in Quito, though some trips can be arranged on the islands at Puerto Ayora. To make sure of seeing a broad selection of wildlife, a stay of up to a week is best. Close to Puerto Ayora is the Charles Darwin Research Station, which houses a museum and an enclosure for the Galapagos land tortoises. More of these can be seen at the tortoise reserve near Santa Rosa in the centre of the island. Although the sheer weight of numbers and the invasive behaviour of some visitors has changed the islands substantially, the Galapagos remain the world's most remarkable natural park.

Gazetteer

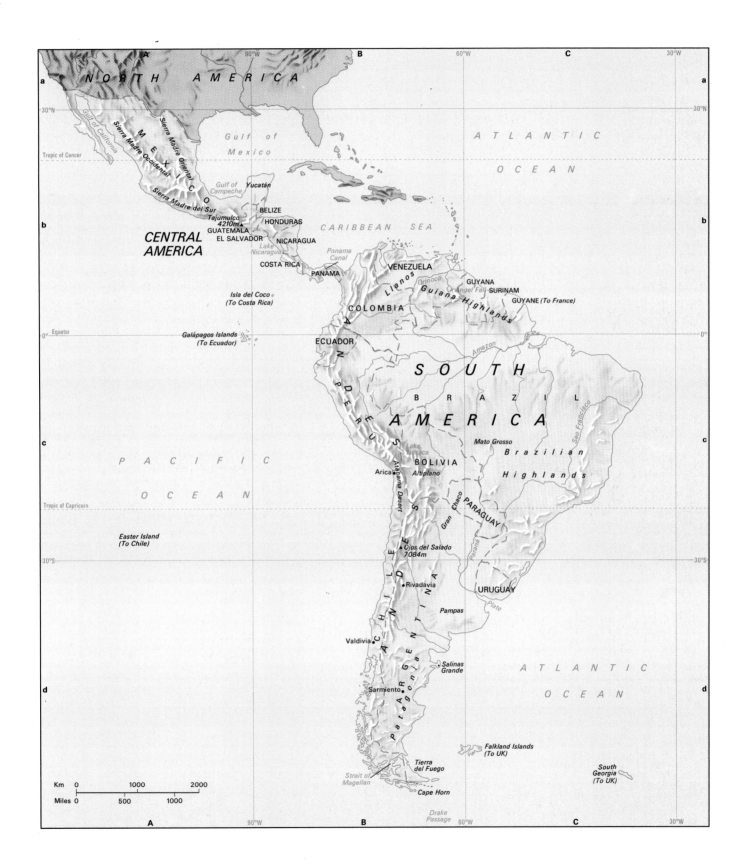

Peru

PERU AT A GLANCE
Area 496,222 square miles
Population 21,905,000
Capital Lima
Government Parliamentary republic
Currency Sol = 100 centavos
Languages Spanish, Quechua, Aymara
Religion Christian (Roman Catholic)
Climate Temperate on coast; cooler in Andes; tropical in selvas. Average temperature in Lima ranges from 13-19°C (55-66°F) in August to 19-28°C (66-82°F) in February
Main primary products Cotton, sugar cane, coffee, rice, potatoes, fruit, vegetables, livestock, fish; crude oil, copper, silver, zinc, lead, iron ore, tungsten
Major industries Agriculture, mining, oil production and refining, fish processing, textiles, cement, leather goods, plastics, chemicals, metal refining, fishing
Main exports Petroleum, copper, sugar, iron ore, silver cotton, zinc, coffee, lead
Annual income per head (US$) 880
Population growth (per thous/yr) 24
Life expectancy (yrs) Male 56 **Female** 60

The lure of gold and silver drew Spanish adventurers down the coast of South America to Peru in the 16th century. The conquistadores *discovered a well-organised Inca empire rich in treasure which they brutally plundered. Mineral wealth made Peru the centrepiece of Spain's empire in America.*

More than half of all Peruvians are Indians. For centuries, many of them were little more than slaves, working in the mines of the Andes for European masters. Mining still plays an important part in Peru's economy, and under the lofty peaks of the Andes lie vast resources of many valuable metals, including copper, silver and iron ore.

Hunters and fishers of early Peru

The first Peruvians migrated from the north, where their ancestors had arrived from Asia some 30,000 years ago over the land bridge which then connected Alaska and Siberia. They were hunters and fishers with primitive weapons of wood, stone and bone. But about 2000 BC agricultural settlements began to spring up, based on the cultivation of beans and squashes – a vegetable like the pumpkin.

Between 300 BC and AD 800, the northern coast of Peru was dominated by the Moche people, who built enormous platforms of sun-dried clay and huge aqueducts and canals up to 75 miles long. They made pottery with modelled and painted scenes showing trees, animals and birds, the weapons used in hunting, and realistic human faces.

The designs of the pottery and textiles of the early Peruvians were affected between AD 500 and 1000 by an important religious influence originating from the bleak plateau near Lake Titicaca, 13,000 feet above sea level, and spreading widely over highland and coast. Artists began to depict a winged god with weeping eyes, carrying a staff in either hand, and attended by figures which represent pumas and condors. This was the creator-god Viracocha, later venerated by the Incas.

The final pre-Inca stage of Peruvian history was between 1000 and 1400, when powerful kingdoms emerged on the coast and in the highlands, and true cities were built. On the north coast, the Chimu, successors to the Moche, had a capital, Chanchan, covering some 8 square miles and made of dried mud-brick. The Chimu built roads and fortresses and had a well-organised state, as did similar kingdoms further south. When the Incas came to power, they learnt much from the peoples they conquered.

The rise and fall of the Inca Empire

No other empire in history had a more dramatic rise and fall than the empire of the Incas. In only 90 years, between 1440 and 1530, it expanded from a small kingdom based on the city of Cuzco to a huge empire including much of present-day Ecuador and stretching southwards through Peru to central Chile. Then, within a few years of reaching its peak, the Inca Empire was torn apart by a small army of European invaders.

In 1438, Pachacuti Inca Yupanqui became Sapa Inca (or emperor), and it was he who began the deliberate expansion of the Inca state, and the policy of absorbing defeated foes into Inca civilisation. He was brilliantly successful, not only in warfare and diplomacy, but also in government and administration, and his heir, his son Topa Inca, had the same kind of organising ability. Between 1438 and the death of Topa in 1493, the Inca Empire was largely established.

The empire's organisation was impressive. After defeating an enemy, the Incas brought in their engineers to construct forts and to extend the communications system. The excellence of the Inca roads gave the armies great mobility, and storehouses of food, clothing and weapons were placed along them at regular intervals – roughly a day's journey apart for a marching man, for the Incas had no wheeled vehicles or horses.

The emperor, the Sapa Inca, was surrounded by veneration and ritual. He was the son of the sun, a living god, and mere mortals entering his presence bowed their heads, went barefoot and carried a small parcel on their backs to symbolise their lowly status in comparison with his divine power.

Seldom have the lives of the mass of the people been so highly organised, from birth to death, as they were under the Incas. This was the society of the ant hill, with thousands of civil servants collecting tribute and administering justice. Trained officials kept the accounts but, since writing was unknown in Inca Peru, they used a system of coloured and knotted cords, quipus, the colours and knots representing commodities and quantities.

All land belonged to the state, and was divided on a three-fold basis: the product of one part supported the court and

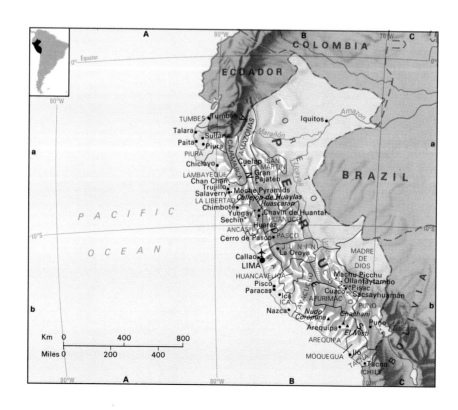

administration; another part paid for the state religion, temples and priesthood; and the third part was divided locally among the people. Taxes were paid in the form of labour, the able-bodied being required to till the lands owned by the state in their own areas before turning to their individual plots.

Privileges and penalties

The rapid expansion of the empire created a large governing class. The Inca nobility, together with chiefs of conquered tribes who had accepted Inca rule, formed the high administration. Their way of life was a less brilliant image of the Sapa Inca's. They lived well at the state's expense, did no manual labour, and had servants and secondary wives.

Nevertheless, status meant responsibility, and Inca laws brought swift and severe punishment on any member of the governing class who failed to do his duty. A noble who committed adultery was sentenced to death, since he had demeaned his class, while a commoner committing the same offence was tortured, but not killed. On the other hand, crimes committed by commoners against the state or against the aristocracy often carried the death penalty. The offender might have his brains beaten out with a club, or be hanged upside-down until dead, thrown from a cliff or stoned to death.

Faith and worship were woven into the daily lives of the Incas. The higher classes believed in Viracocha, the shadowy creator-god who had made all things, including the heavenly bodies. Viracocha was so great a force, inhabiting the whole universe, that only one temple, near the capital, was dedicated to his name, and only the court and the high nobility were allowed to worship him.

The empire had imposing temples in many places, particularly in provincial capitals, but none matched the great sun temple at Cuzco, called Coricancha, or the 'House of Gold'. This temple, made of perfectly shaped rectangular blocks of stone, contained a huge disc of solid gold representing the sun.

Human sacrifice was rare in the Inca Empire, though it was practised at times of great national crisis, such as the illness of the emperor, plague or famine. The victims were usually children, ten-year-old boys and girls chosen for their perfect physique and appearance; they were killed by strangulation or by cutting their throats.

A doom foretold

This confident, expanding empire of 12 million people was about to suffer a shock before which it was utterly defenceless, like a human body attacked by some strange and irresistible virus. Late in December 1530, a Spanish force of 180 men sailed southwards from Panama. Their commander, Francisco Pizarro, an illiterate but experienced soldier, knew precisely what he was after, for in 1528 he had voyaged along the Inca coastline and seen something of the empire's riches.

His task appeared a hard one. The Inca Empire had been created by the best military machine in ancient America, and its communications were good. But the Spaniards arrived in the wake of a civil war which split the empire. The Sapa Inca, Huayna Capac, died about 1525 and the succession was disputed between his sons Atahualpa and Huascar. Atahualpa, with the aid of the best Inca generals, defeated Huascar in battle and became emperor. But the realm had suffered an enormous shock and had not yet settled down when Pizarro reached Tumbes in 1532.

Other factors favoured the Spaniards. Being so few, they had nothing to lose and everything to gain, and they fought with a savage ruthlessness. Moreover, while the Inca armies were superb at their own technological level, firearms and weapons of steel were a different matter. The Spanish horses were an unknown terror: the first Indians to see an unhorsed Spaniard fled, believing that a strange animal had come apart to form two separate beings.

Finally, Inca lore had long forecast that the god Viracocha would return one day to his kingdom; some legends said that the god was light-skinned. When white strangers arrived, with weapons that made thunder and lightning, the psychological impact was immense. Pizarro murdered Atahualpa and captured Cuzco. The Inca Empire disappeared, and its people became subjects of a new Sapa Inca across the seas.

After that, Peru rapidly became the most important Spanish territory in the New World. Lima, the country's present capital, was established in 1535 as the seat of government for Spain's possessions in South America, except Venezuela.

Republican Peru

José de San Martín proclaimed Peru's independence in 1821 when he forced the Spanish viceroy to flee Lima. But it was not until 1826 that all troops loyal to Spain surrendered. In 1864 Spain, which had never recognised Peru's independence, seized the Chinca islands, rich in guano fertiliser – Peru's main source of wealth at that time. Joined by its neighbours, Chile, Ecuador and Bolivia, Peru declared war on Spain. Peace was not made until 1879, when Spain formally recognised Peru's independence.

A territorial war with Chile, settled in 1929, cost Peru two nitrate-producing provinces. A modest financial recovery began later, but Peru's frequent changes from civilian governments to military regimes have hampered economic progress. In 1968 the constitutional democracy of Fernando Belaúnde Terry was ousted by General Juan Velasco Alvarado, who set up a 'social proprietorship' of industry, commerce and agriculture. Known as the Inca Plan, it was to put Peru under collective management. However, in 1977, the plan was reversed to restore private enterprise under a new military regime, which had very different priorities. With 13,000 infants dying annually from malnutrition, the military spent $140 million for supersonic fighter-bombers.

In 1980, after 18 years of military rule, Belaúnde campaigned on a slogan of 'Peru for the Peruvians' and was returned to the presidency of a nation on the verge of bankruptcy. Belaúnde's government received help from international loan agencies to finance a five-year development plan for 1981-5 to develop agriculture, transportation, and public services.

Although Peru's economy grew at a higher rate than most other South American countries in 1980-2, lower prices for oil, copper, and silver cut government revenues and forced Belaúnde to reduce capital developments. About half of Peru's workers were unemployed or underemployed in 1982-3, and inflation continued at a rate of 50 per cent. The Peruvian economy slid into depression in 1983 as drought in the south hurt farm production and floods in the north caused widespread damage and destruction. At the same time, the Maoist Sendero Luminoso (Shining Path) guerrilla movement gathered widespread support among the shanty towns around the country's major cities and the Indians of the highlands.

In 1985, the populist left-winger Alán García Pérez was elected president, but achieved little in bringing either the economy of the Shining Path guerrillas under control. His successor, elected in 1990, was the right-winger Alberto Fujimori, a Peruvian of Japanese descent, with strong commitments to free-market policies. In April 1992, he dissolved Congress and suspended the constitution, claiming that he needed more freedom to pursue his economic reforms and to carry on the fight against drugs traffickers (another growing problem) and Shining Path terrorism.

VENEZUELA AT A GLANCE
Area 352,143 square miles
Population 19,698,000
Capital Caracas
Government Parliamentary republic
Currency Bolívar = 100 céntimos
Language Spanish
Religion Christian (95% Roman Catholic, 2% Protestant)
Climate Tropical; humid lowlands; cooling progressively with altitude. Temperature at Caracas averages 24-27°C (75-81°F) all year. Los Nevados (village in Andes) constantly cold: 14°C (57°F). Rainy season May to November
Main primary products Livestock, coffee, cocoa, maize, rice, sugar, cotton, tobacco, fruit, vegetables; petroleum, iron ore, diamonds, manganese, bauxite (aluminium ore), gold, coal
Major industries Steel, transport, equipment, ships, petroleum products, chemicals, food processing, textiles, cement, aluminium
Main exports Crude oil and products
Annual income per head (US$) 2700
Population growth (per thous/yr) 30
Life expectancy (yrs) Male 66 **Female** 70

Venezuela

Oil has made Venezuela one of the most prosperous Latin American countries. It is a leading oil-exporting nation and it is also one of the world's 10 most important producers of iron ore – though in recent years falls in oil prices and one of the largest foreign debts in the world have somewhat dented the country's wealth.

Rule by Spain

When Christopher Columbus discovered Venezuela in 1498, it was inhabited by different groups of Carib and Arawak Indians. Unlike their counterparts in many other South American countries, they left no evidence of great pre-Columbian civilisations. Venezuela now has one of the smallest Indian populations in the continent – about 150,000, roughly 1 per cent of the total population. The few Indians who remain include the Yanomani who live in the country's Amazonian hinterland, and the Bari who live in the north-west, near the border with Colombia.

The Spanish made their first coastal settlement in Venezuela at Cumaná in 1520; the future capital Caracas was founded in 1567. Venezuela was also the reputed site of the fabled golden city of El Dorado and drew other European adventurers, anxious to make a quick fortune. The Elizabethan Englishman Sir Walter Raleigh, in particular, twice sailed up the Orinoco river in a vain search for El Dorado.

Venezuela remained part of the Spanish empire until the early 19th century, but many Venezuelans – including many of its creole (white) inhabitants – became increasingly restive under the colonial regime. There were three uprisings during the 18th century, and in 1806 and again in 1811 the creole landowner Francisco Miranda led bids for independence. Miranda was eventually captured by the Spanish authorities, but the fight was carried on by one of his former lieutenants, Simón Bolívar – a creole like Miranda, though with some Indian blood.

Bolívar the Great Liberator

Bolívar had some early successes, but these proved short-lived, especially after the defeat of Napoleon in Europe allowed the Spanish to send more forces to South America. In 1815, Bolívar fled into exile on the British West Indian island of Jamaica. From 1817, however, his fortunes began to mend. He returned to Venezuela, establishing himself at Angostura (now Ciudad Bolívar) at the mouth of the Orinoco.

With vital reinforcements from a contingent of British veterans of the Napoleonic Wars, he set out on a march across the Andes into what is now Colombia. In 1819 his army won the battle of Boyacá and captured the Colombian capital Bogatá. Back in Venezuela, a revolutionary congress meeting at Angostura proclaimed a new and independent republic,

Gran Colombia, comprising modern Venezuela, Colombia, Panama and Ecuador. In 1821, a revolutionary army managed to defeat the last major Spanish army in Venezuela at Carabobo.

Bolívar was determined to preserve the unity of Gran Colombia, but many Venezuelans, led by General José Antonio Páez, wanted to go it alone. Páez and his partisans eventually prevailed, and in 1829 Venezuela proclaimed itself an independent republic, with Páez as its president. The next year, a disillusioned Bolívar, broken in health, decided to abandon South America for renewed exile – in Europe. In the event, he never got that far. Aged just 47, he died of tuberculosis on December 17, 1830, on a country estate belonging to a friend near Santa Marta in Colombia.

Dictators and oil

Venezuela had suffered more than any other South American country in the struggle for independence. Its economy was ruined and almost a quarter of its population was killed. Throughout the rest of the 19th century, the country was ruled by a series of corrupt dictators.

In 1908 Juan Vicente Gómez seized power. His position was strengthened by the discovery of oil in vast quantities in 1918. Oil revenues enabled Gómez to pay all Venezuela's foreign debts and also to modernise the army and secret police. Today he is referred to as El Benemérito, 'The Deserving', in ironic comment on his greed and ruthlessness. After Gómez's death in 1935 the army's leaders continued to hold power. They were overthrown, however, in 1945 by a group of liberal-minded junior officers, who installed a civilian government.

The civilian experiment

The country's new civilian leaders, Rómulo Betancourt and Rómulo Gallegos, tried to modernise Venezuela and turn it into a welfare state. But their policies antagonised the rich, who overthrew them in 1948. By 1953 power had passed into the hands of Marcos Pérez Jiménez. He won US support through his anti-Communist measures, but his dictatorship was overthrown in 1958 and Betancourt returned.

In 1969 Rafael Caldera of the Christian Social Party (COPEI) became the first opposition candidate to win power democratically. He tried to conciliate the Left and reduce the power of Communist guerrillas. In the 1970s, President Carlos Andrés Pérez ruled during a period of unprecedented prosperity for Venezuela, thanks to rises in oil prices. The Democratic Action Party leader Jaime Lusinchi won the presidency by a wide margin in December 1983, defeating former president Caldera. After taking office in February 1984, Lusinchi announced a comprehensive programme to revive the country's stagnating economy and deal with its mounting foreign debt, which had more than tripled during the previous five years. In 1989, Carlos Andrés Pérez was elected for a second term as president.

Colombia

The growth of Colombia has been marked by some of the most bitter struggles experienced by any country in South America. In the 70 years up to 1903 the country was ravaged by 27 civil wars, while in the first half of the present century, hundreds of thousands were killed in strife between political factions. More recently, the activities of the country's cocaine traffickers have resulted in still more violence.

Colombia is a land of snow-capped peaks, vast lowland pastures and torrid jungles, still inhabited in some regions along the Venezuelan border by Indians leading an untouched traditional life. Similar peoples occupied much of Colombia when Spanish explorers arrived in 1499. In the region around the modern capital Bogotá, they included the Chibca Indians whose society was organised on a more sophisticated basis than that of many of their neighbours. Each district had its own chief, and each belonged to one of two larger states, ruled over by a series of hereditary princes. The Chibca (or Muisca) Indians were also fine goldsmiths, whose work can today be seen in Bogotá's Gold Museum.

The Spanish, when they arrived, found valuable gold deposits, and between 1525 and 1533 they established the first settlements at Santa Marta and Cartagena on the Caribbean coast. Cartagena later became one of the most important ports in Spanish America, formidably defended with a string of forts and massive walls. It is here that the Spanish treasure fleets assembled before making the journey back to Spain. This also made Cartegena a tempting target for free-roaming pirates and the like – including the Elizabethan English buccaneer Sir Francis Drake. Bogotá, meanwhile, was founded in 1538, and became a lively cultural centre, known as 'the Athens of South America'.

New Granada becomes independent

Bogotá was the capital of the Spanish viceroyalty of New Granada, which included parts of present-day Panama, Venezuela and Ecuador, as well as most of Colombia.

At the end of the 18th century, the French Revolution in faraway Europe left its mark on New Granada. In 1794, a local translation was made of the revolutionary French Declaration of the Rights of Man, which served as inspiration to many creole (white) Colombians who were becoming increasingly restive with Spanish rule. This bore fruit in 1810 when a group of revolutionaries in Bogotá proclaimed their independence from Spain. Their example was followed by similar groups (or

juntas) set up elsewhere in Colombia. In 1813, the Colombian revolutionaries were joined by the Venezuelan Simón Bolívar, who won a series of victories against the Spanish before returning to Venezuela where his successes were eventually checked at Caracas.

With the fall of Napoleon in Europe in 1815, Spain was able to concentrate more resources on South America. General Pablo Morillo reconquered Cartagena after an 106-day siege and in 1816 instituted a punitive 'Reign of Terror' in Bogotá in an attempt to stamp out the revolutionaries. The next year, however, Bolívar struck back. Advancing on Colombia across the Andes from Venezuela, he defeated the Spanish at the battle of the Swamps of Vargas in July 1819 and at Boyacá in August. He then took Bogotá. In December, a congress meeting at Angostura in Venezuela proclaimed the new republic of Gran Colombia, including modern Colombia, Venezuela, Panama and Ecuador, with Bolívar as president.

In the end Gran Colombia lasted only 10 years. Bolívar fought hard to preserve the union, but Venezuela split off in 1829 and Ecuador in 1830. The rump, consisting of modern Colombia and Panama, returned to the old name of New Granada, officially adopting the name Colombia only in 1863.

Liberals and Conservatives

By the end of the 19th century, two strongly opposed political parties had developed in Colombia – the Conservatives who wanted a strong, centralised government and close ties with the Roman Catholic Church; and the Liberals who wanted less government control and a separation of the state from the Church. The strength of these parties was almost equal, and no caudillo (strong man) emerged.

Political strife and civil unrest followed. One civil war was followed by another; guerrilla and bandit groups flourished, and the economy was disrupted. The particularly bloody War of the Thousand Days, between Liberal and Conservative forces, broke out in 1899, and by the time of the eventual Conservative victory in 1902, 100,000 lives had been lost. In 1903 Colombia lost Panama, which proclaimed itself an independent republic.

Coffee: the economic mainstay

Helped by an increased world demand for its coffee, Colombia was able to progress towards stability in the 30 years up to 1948. Coffee-processing industries were expanded, and steel and textile mills started. But the assassination of the Liberal leader Jorge Eliécer Gaitán in 1948 plunged the country back into a nine-year period of chaos, known as La Violencia, during which an estimated 300,000 people lost their lives. Riots

COLOMBIA AT A GLANCE

Area 456,535 square miles

Population 33,076,000

Capital Bogotá

Government Republic

Currency Peso = 100 centavos

Language Spanish

Religion Christian (97% Roman Catholic, 1% Protestant)

Climate Tropical on coast, temperate on plateaus. Average temperature in Bogotá (altitude 8563 ft) ranges from 10-18°C (50-64°F) in July to 9-20°C (48-68°F) in February

Main primary products Coffee, rice, potatoes, cassava, sugar, bananas, maize, cattle, timber; oil and natural gas, emeralds, platinum, gold, silver, iron ore, coal

Major industries Agriculture, mining, iron and steel, food processing, cement, oil refining, paper, textiles

Main exports Coffee, textiles and clothing, fruit and vegetables, sugar, chemicals, cotton, machinery

Annual income per head (US$) 1110

Population growth (per thous/yr) 21

Life expectancy (yrs) Male 61 **Female** 65

and crime were met with violent rule, under such men as Gustavo Rojas Pinilla. Some semblance of order was restored in 1958 with the election of a moderate Liberal leader, Alberto Lleras Camargo, and an agreement that the Conservatives and Liberals would take the presidency in alternate four-year terms until 1974. A new political movement, however, emerged in the late 1960s, backed by Rojas Pinilla. Rojas was defeated for the presidency in 1970 by the Conservative Misael Pastrana Borrero.

The first free elections in more than two decades were held in 1974. A Liberal, Alfonso López Michelsen, was elected president; his four-year term was marred by widespread corruption. Liberal rule ended in 1982 with the election of Conservative Belisario Betancur to the presidency. Violence

has been a part of Colombian life since the 1940s and one of Betancur's first moves as president was to offer an amnesty to left-wing guerrillas. Although hundreds accepted the amnesty, fighting continued and in 1984 the government signed truce agreements with three guerrilla groups in a new effort to end violence.

In 1986, Betancur was succeeded by the Liberal Virgilio Barco, who was followed in turn by his fellow Liberal César Gaviria Trujillo after elections in 1990. Violence continued to dog the country, with added impetus from the cocaine-trafficking cartels, such as the notorious Medellín cartel headed by Pablo Escobar. Despite massive support from the United States, attempts to stamp out the drug trade failed to have much effect.

Bolivia

The remote and mountainous republic of Bolivia has had its full share of the violent upheavals that have marked the history of South America. During the past 450 years its lands have been plundered for minerals. Its boundaries have been eroded by a succession of disastrous wars, its people crushed by poverty and social inequalities; and military coups have wrecked attempts to create a stable government, frequently bringing the country to the brink of bankruptcy.

Aymaras and Incas
The Aymaras, a farming race descended from peoples who crossed the Bering Strait from Asia to North America more than 30,000 years ago, established the first important civilisation in modern Bolivia around 1000 BC. They worshipped the creator-god Viracocha – later adopted by the Incas – and their craftsmen created fine pottery, textiles and metalwork. They also built impressive temple complexes, including one whose ruins survive at Tiahuanaco in north-west Bolivia. This was probably Viracocha's major shrine. Huge stone figures, granite pillars, terraced courts and stone-lined enclosures cover the site today, and a gateway is embossed with a frieze of a weeping god; his tears may symbolise rain.

Around AD 900, the Aymaras suffered an unknown catastrophe, and when the Incas from Peru arrived in the region around Tiahuanaco and the neighbouring Lake Titicaca in about AD 1200, the local people had only the dimmest memories of their former glories. They were tough fighters, none the less, so that it took the Incas 200 years before they were able to subdue the Aymaras fully. Only a few decades after that, in the 1530s, the Incas were themselves overthrown when the conquistador Francisco Pizarro, with his brothers Gonzalo, Juan and Hernando, led the Spanish conquest of Peru.

Spanish explorers followed, searching for minerals. They found wealth far in excess of their dreams in the mountains of the Andes. The huge silver deposits discovered in 1546 at Potosí were the richest the world had ever known, and by 1650 Potosí was the largest city in the New World, with a population of 160,000. The region's native Indian peoples were forced to work the silver mines, under conditions of extreme hardship.

Shrinking boundaries: 1879-1935
The people of Bolivia – then known as Upper Peru – were among the first in South America to seek independence from Spain, although in the end they were the last to achieve it. In 1809, teachers and students at the University of St Francis Xavier in Chuquisaca (now Sucre) led calls for the independence of all the South American colonies, and there were uprisings that year at both Chuquisaca and La Paz. Freedom came only in 1825, however. The previous year, Antonion José de Sucre – one of the ablest generals serving under the Venezuelan-born 'Great Liberator', Simón Bolívar –

had defeated the Spanish at Ayacucho in Peru. He then invaded Bolivia, winning a final victory over the Spanish at Tumusla. On August 25, 1825, Bolívar officially named the new republic after himself.

Bolivia then covered an area more than two-and-a-half times its present size, with a sea coast on the western, Pacific side of the continent. This coastal region, which included the rich nitrate and copper deposits of the Atacama Desert, was seized by Chile in the War of the Pacific (1879-84).

Bolivia's riches tempted other neighbours, too. Brazil took over the rubber-tree state of the Amazonas in the south-west in 1903, and Paraguay claimed further lands in the Chaco War (1932-5). During this war, a new generation of young and educated revolutionaries emerged in Bolivia. Internal strife increased. Coup followed coup, each one further weakening the country's economy.

For most of its independent history Bolivia has endured factional strife and military dictatorship. In 1952 there emerged a powerful new regime led by Victor Paz Estenssoro, a lawyer and professor of economics, and backed by the revolutionaries of the Chaco War. Under Paz Estenssoro, drastic reforms were introduced. The Indian majority of the population was given more equal rights, land was shared, foreign-controlled mines nationalised and industries modernised with massive financial aid from the United States. But Bolivia lacked the skilled technicians and the up-to-date equipment to complete the industrial reforms; and attempts to develop roads and social services failed. Strikes plagued the economy and financial chaos followed.

Bolivia today
Paz Estenssoro was overthrown in 1964. A guerrilla campaign against the government started in 1967 with guidance from Che Guevara, a chief lieutenant in the 1956 invasion of Cuba

BOLIVIA AT A GLANCE
Area 424,163 square miles

Population 6,707,000

Capital La Paz

Government Parliamentary republic

Currency Peso = 100 centavos

Languages Spanish, Quechua, Aymara

Religion Christian (95% Roman Catholic)

Climate Tropical; cooler at altitude. Average temperature in La Paz ranges from 1-17°C (34-63°F) in July to 6-19° (43-66°F) in November

Main primary products Potatoes, maize, sugar cane, rice, cassava, coffee, llamas, alpacas; tin, oil and natural gas, copper, lead, zinc, antimony, bismuth, tungsten, silver, gold, sulphur, iron

Major industries Mining and smelting, oil and gas production, textiles, handicrafts, food processing, cement

Main exports Tin, antimony, tungsten, zinc, silver, lead, natural gas

Annual income per head (US$) 660

Population growth (per thous/yr) 26

Life expectancy (yrs) Male 49 **Female** 53

which brought Fidel Castro to power. Guerrilla activities waned after Guevara was killed in Bolivia in 1967.

Bolivia's recent history has been marked by political instability, repression and widespread strikes, resulting in economic crisis. From 1969 to 1982, Bolivia was under military rule, interrupted by popular dissension and protest, questionable elections, failed military coups, and interim presidents selected by the Congress. In 1982 a civilian government was restored with Hernan Siles Zuazo, a former president, as its head. He inherited an annual inflation rate of 150 per cent and an almost bankrupt treasury. In 1983, the worst drought in the nation's history destroyed most of Bolivia's crops and forced the government to import food to prevent mass starvation.

Faced with a series of general strikes by labour unions demanding increases in wages and a deteriorating economic situation, Siles Zuazo called general elections in 1985. None of the 18 presidential candidates won the required 50 per cent of the vote, and the new president was chosen by the Congress, which selected former President Victor Paz Estenssoro. Paz Estenssoro promised to encourage foreign investment, renegotiate the country's foreign debt, crack down on cocaine trafficking (Bolivia is a main supplier to the international narcotics market) and eliminate corruption.

Elections in 1989 were again inconclusive, and Congress again had to make the final selection. The eventual winner was Jaime Paz Zamora of the Movement of the Revolutionary Left (MIR, after he made a surprising deal with the former military dictator General Hugo Banzer) – Banzer was allowed to nominate a number of members of the government.

Chile

Before 1973, Chile was noted for its traditions of peaceful democratic change, which made it a rarity in a continent where change usually spells violent revolution. In 1970 it became the only state outside Europe with a democratically elected Marxist government. But the radical measures speedily imposed by the new leader President Allende in his 'socialist experiment' antagonised many Chileans and their allies abroad. In September 1973 Allende's regime came to a violent end.

Inca setbacks
The Incas added northern Chile to their empire in the mid-15th century, but received one of their rare setbacks (before the Spanish conquest) when they encountered the fierce Araucanian Indians – particularly the warriors of the Mapuche people – of the south. Spanish conquistadores in turn occupied northern Chile in 1533 after conquering the Incas. But an attempt in 1536 to extend Spanish territory southwards similarly met with fierce resistance from the Araucanian Indians, who in the end were not completely subdued until 1880.

In 1541 Pedro de Valdivia founded Santiago, the capital of Chile. It was a further 200 years before Spain completed its occupation of present-day Chile down the long coastal strip south of the River Bío-Bío. Finding little mineral wealth there, the Spanish developed an agricultural society.

An Irishman's son becomes president
With the decline of Spanish power throughout South America, Chilean patriots rose against their Spanish overlords in the early 19th century. They were lead by Bernardo O'Higgins, the Chilean-born son of an Irishman, and José de San Martín. Chile proclaimed its independence in 1818, and O'Higgins became the first president of the new nation.

The constitution of 1833, which paved the way for parliamentary government, remained virtually unchanged until 1925. With internal stability, Chile prospered, though agriculture remained backward. In 1884, the country emerged from the five-year War of the Pacific against Bolivia and Peru with vast new riches – the mineral deposits of the northern Atacama lands won from its defeated enemies. The most important minerals in this rain-free desert were nitrates and copper.

The value of nitrates to Europe as a fertiliser transformed Chile's economy at the turn of the century. When this boom came to an end after the First World War, a second period of prosperity for Chile followed with the development of copper mining.

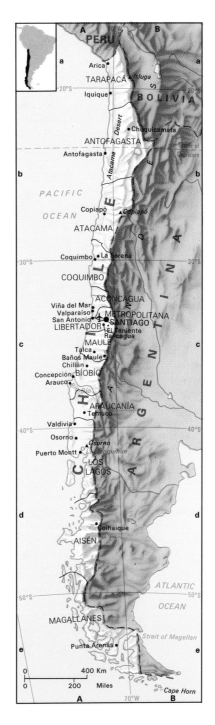

CHILE AT A GLANCE

Area 292,256 square miles

Population 13,082,000

Capital Santiago

Government Parliamentary republic

Currency Peso = 1000 escudos

Language Spanish

Religion Christian (90% Roman Catholic)

Climate Varies from dry desert in the north to subarctic in the south. Average temperature in Santiago ranges from 3-14°C (37-57°F) in July to 12-29°C (54-84°F) in January

Main primary products Wheat, maize, rice, sugar beet, potatoes, beans, timber, fruit, grapes, fish; copper, coal, iron, nitrates, molybdenum, zinc, manganese, lead, oil

Major industries Steel, cellulose and wood pulp, cement, food processing, ceramics, glass, forestry, fishing

Main exports Copper, paper and wood pulp, iron ore, nitrates, wine, fruit, fishmeal, processed fish

Annual income per head (US$) 1970

Population growth (per thous/yr) 15

Life expectancy (yrs) Male 65 **Female** 70

A Marxist experiment

Unemployment and political unrest brought Chile to the verge of revolution in the 1920s, but this was avoided when President Arturo Alessandri Palma, who had the support of the working and middle classes, introduced labour reforms and a new constitution in 1925. From then until 1970, despite a period of severe inflation in the 1950s, the economy remained stable. The country suffered a major setback in 1960 when a disastrous earthquake razed entire cities.

In 1970, Dr Salvador Allende Gossens became president. His Marxist coalition government soon ran into difficulties. Its nationalisation programme, particularly of foreign-owned businesses, led to tension with the United States, controller of much of Chile's copper interests. Former US President Richard Nixon revealed in 1976 that he had ordered the CIA to try to prevent Allende's election.

Allende's government also alienated middle-class Chileans, who in 1972 combined in an employer's 'strike' against the government. Inflation, pressure from left-wing extremists, and peasant opposition to state planning added to the difficulties.

Allende was killed during a military coup in 1973; General Augusto Pinochet Ugarte took over and purged thousands of Allende supporters – at least 2500 were summarily executed;
thousands were imprisoned without trial; 30,000 were exiled. US military aid was cut off in 1975 because of human rights violations. There were further crackdowns on government opponents in 1980.

There was a shift to a a free-market economy in 1975 when 400 state-owned businesses were sold off. Production picked up and inflation was reduced from 600 per cent to 10 per cent in 4 years. However, in 1982-3 Chile was hit by falling copper prices and a world recession; unemployment rose to 25 per cent and many businesses went bankrupt.

Democracy returns

From 1983 there was a rising tide of protest – calls for Pinochet's resignation, regular anti-government demonstrations, and a national strike to protest against the continuation of military rule. In 1989, these bore fruit in presidential and congressional elections and in March 1990 the moderate Christian Democrat Patricio Aylwin Azócar took office as president in a peaceful transfer of power – although Pinochet remained Army Commander. Since then, much effort has been put into healing the wounds of the past 20 years, particularly in repealing the repressive measures put into place by the military.

Ecuador

Crossed by the Equator, from which it takes its name, Ecuador was one of the poorest states of South America until the development of its petroleum industry in the 1970s. Much of the country's life is still dominated by a small aristocracy and by the Roman Catholic Church. Its capital Quito is also one of the most attractive in the continent, with narrow cobbled streets, fine Spanish colonial architecture and a magnificent mountain setting, overlooked by the 15,728-foot volcanic cone of Mount Pichincha.

Capital of the northern Incas

The original Indian inhabitants of Ecuador had reached a high level of culture before they were conquered at the end of the 15th century by the Inca Empire, to the south. For a while, the Incas made Quito joint capital of their empire, along with Cuzco in Peru. But Inca rule was overthrown in less than a century by Spanish conquistadores.

In 1534, Peru's conqueror Francisco Pizarro sent two of his lieutenants Sebastián de Benalcázar and Diego de Almagro to capture Quito, which later became one of the most important cities in the Spanish Viceroyalty of Peru. It was also from Ecuador that another conquistador, Francisco de Orellana, set off in 1541 down the Napo river in a search for gold and silver. In the event, he followed the river until it joined the Amazon and followed that until it reached the Atlantic. He thus became the first European to cross the width of South America and explore the Amazon basin.

Ecuador settled down reasonably peacefully to Spanish rule. Many of the native Indians became slaves on tobacco and sugar plantations, but the mingling of Spanish art forms with local crafts skills inherited from the Incas also produced a remarkable flowering of the arts. Ecuadorean painting, sculpture and architecture during the colonial period was among the finest on the continent.

Independence and dictatorship

In 1809, an attempted uprising in Quito against Spanish rule was swiftly quelled, and Ecuador had to wait another 13 years before winning independence. This they owed to the Venezuelan Antonio José de Sucre. In 1822, South America's Great Liberator Simón Bolívar sent Sucre by sea from Colombia to seize Ecuador's chief port Guayaquico, where local patriots had already started a rebellion against the

Spanish at the battle of Mount Pichincha. Ecuador initially formed part of Bolívar's republic of Gran Colombia, including modern Colombia, Panama and Venezuela, but when this broke up in 1830 Ecuador became fully independent.

After 1830 the country suffered nearly 30 years of civil war. Two factions fought for power – the Conservatives, led by Juan José Flores until his exile in 1845, and the Liberals. In 1860, after a disastrous war with Peru, the Conservative leader, Gabriel García Moreno, a religious fanatic, seized power. His dictatorial rule lasted until his assassination in 1876.

After two more decades of unrest and disorder, another revolution brought the Liberal leader Eloy Alfaro to power in 1895. Successive Liberal presidents held office until 1944. They curbed the power of the Church and established a measure of civil liberty. But after 1944 political rivalries and the intervention of the army resulted in frequent changes in the government.

Ecuador's longest period of political stability was under Galo Plaza Lasso from 1948 to 1955. Plaza, the first of Ecuador's presidents to survive for a full term of office, was succeeded by José María Velasco Ibarra, who within a year brought Ecuador to the brink of war with neighbouring Peru.

Velasco was driven from office in 1956, but returned to power in 1960 and, after an interim of army rule, again in 1968. The military seized power in 1972 to forestall scheduled elections and to seek control of Ecuador's oil wealth, opened up by a 313-mile pipeline across the Andes. After seven years of military rule, a new constitution was proclaimed in 1978, and presidential elections were held in April 1979. They were won by lawyer Jaime Roldós Aguilera. His first struggle in the move towards democracy was to win support from a unicameral congress and the legislature.

Roldós was killed in a plane crash in 1981. His successor was the Vice President Osvaldo Hurtado Larrea, head of the moderate Popular Democracy Party. Because of lower oil prices, his government had to bring in tough economic measures that caused strikes and demonstrations. The 1984 presidential election was won by the conservative León Febres Cordero. His strongly free-market policies led to defeat, however, in elections in 1988. He was succeeded by the centre-left Rodrigo Borja Cevallos, and then, after a fresh round of elections in 1992, by Sixto Duran Bellén of the Party of Republican Unity.

ECUADOR AT A GLANCE

Area 109,483 square miles
Population 10,506,000
Capital Quito
Government Parliamentary republic
Currency Sucre = 100 centavos
Languages Spanish, Indian languages
Religion Christian (96% Roman Catholic, 2% Protestant)
Climate Tropical; cooler at altitude. Average temperature in Quito (altitude 9350 ft) ranges from 8°C (46°F) to 21°C (70°F)
Main primary products Rice, maize, cassava, potatoes, bananas, oranges, coffee, cocoa, sugar cane, fish; crude oil and natural gas
Major industries Agriculture, crude oil production and refining, cement, petrochemicals, food processing
Main exports Crude oil, cocoa and products, bananas, coffee, processed fish
Annual income per head (US$) 935
Population growth (per thous/yr) 27
Life expectancy (yrs) Male 60 **Female** 64

1 CHIMBORAZO
2 BOLIVAR
3 TUNGURAHUA

Picture Credits

p.9 F. Hidalgo; p.10 Larrain-Magnum; p.11 Schoenahl-Diaf; p.12 Régent-A. Hutchison Lby; p.13 Boireau-Rapho; p.14 Sioen-Cedri; p.15 top Sioen-Cedri; bottom Sioen-Cedri; p.16 Adamini-Gamma; p.17 A. Hutchison Lby; p.18 S. Held p.19 left F. Kohler; right S. Held; p.20 Doublet-Pix; p.21 top Desjardins-Explorer; bottom Doublet-Pix; p.22 S. Held; p.23 top F. Kohler; bottom D. Jeu; p.24 Silvester-Rapho; p.25 left du Authier-Fotogram; right Duchêne-Diaf; p.26 top F. Hidalgo; bottom Vogel-Rapho; p.27 A. Hutchison Lby; p.28 D. Jeu; p.29 F. Bouillot-Marco-Polo; p.30 F. Kohler; p.31 F. Bouillot-Marco-Polo; p.32 M. Bruggmann; p.33 M. Bruggmann; p.34 F. Bouillot-Marco-Polo; p.35 left F. Hidalgo; right F. Bouillot-Marco-Polo; p.36 B. Régent-A. Hutchison Lby; p.37 Bellenger-Lada Production; p.38 C. Collin Delavaud; p.39 C. Lénars; p.40 F. Hidalgo; p.41 top Silvester-Rapho; bottom C. Lénars; p.42 F. Hidalgo; p.43 top F. Hidalgo; bottom F. Hidalgo; p.44 left Vincent-Rapho; right Mathieu-Rapho; p.45 Guillou-Atlas-Photo; p.46 Rozencwajg-Atlas-Photo; p.47 left Truchet-Fotogram; right A. Hutchison Lby; p.48 C. Lénars; p.49 Boutin-Atlas-Photo; p.50 top Kerjean-Rastoin; bottom Sioen-Cedri; p.52 Sioen-Cedri; p.53 Sioen-Cedri; p.54 top Boutin-Explorer; bottom Sioen-Cedri; p.55 Phillips-Image Bank; p.56 Boutin-Vloo; p.57 top Sioen-Cedri; bottom Robillard; p.58 Mattison-Gamma; p.59 left Kerjean-Rastion; right Kerjean-Rastion; p.60 Sioen-Cedri; p.60/61 de Steinheil-Rapho; p.61 Sioen-Cedri; p.62 Sioen-Cedri; p.63 top Sioen-Cedri; bottom Kerjean-Rastion; p.64 Gladu-Atlas-Photo; p.65 Taurines-Explorer; p.66 top Sioen-Cedri; bottom Sioen-Cedri; p.67 Sioen-Cedri; p.68 Rousseau-Top; p.69 M. Bruggmann; p.70 Frey-Image Bank; p.71 left; A. Hutchison Lby; right Cagnoni-Rapho; p.72 Hinous-Top; p.73 Stevens-Atlas-Photo; p.74 A. Hutchison Lby;

p.75 A. Hutchison Lby; p.76 A. Hutchison Lby; p.77 Maisel-Image Bank; p.78 Moser-A. Hutchison Lby; p.79 left A. Hutchison Lby; right A. Hutchison Lby; p.80 Vuillomenet-Rapho; p.81 left Abbas-Gamma; right N. Daguet; p.82 Orive-Gamma; p.83 left A. Hutchison Lby; right Martel-Gamma; p.84 Spiegel-Rapho; p.85 left M. Bruggmann; right Moser-A. Hutchison Lby; p.86 Frey-Image Bank; p.86/87 A. Hutchison Lby; p.87 Moser A. Hutchison Lby; p.88 Frey-Image Bank; p.89 Salgado-Gamma; p.90 top Adamini-Gamma; bottom M. Bruggmann; p.92 M. Bruggmann; p.93 left Salgado-Gamma; right Desjardins-Top; p.94 Silvester Rapho; p.95 top Silvester-Rapho; bottom Adamini-Gamma; p.96 left Torregano-Explorer; right Kérébel-Diaf; p.97 left Détrez-Pix; right Gamma; p.98 left Adamini-Gamma; right M. Bruggmann; p.99 Moser-A. Hutchison Lby; p.100 top Desjardins-Top; bottom Lozouet-Image Bank; p.101 F.Kohler; p.102 top left Auvray-Explorer; bottom left Auvray-Explorer; top right F. Kohler; bottom right F. Kohler; p.103 F. Kohler; p.104 F. Kohler; p.105 F. Kohler; p.106 Schoenahl-Diaf; p.107 left Serraillier-Rapho; right Adamini-Gamma; p.108 M. Bruggmann; p.109 Duchêne-Diaf; p.110 top Duchêne-Diaf; bottom Depardon-Magnum; p.111 Larrain-Magnum; p.112 Sioen-Cedri; p.113 left Sioen-Cedri; right Sioen-Cedri; p.114 A. Hutchison Lby; p.115 Sioen-Cedri; p.116 Depardon-Magnum; p.117 Depardon-Magnum; p.118 top Robillard; bottom Sioen-Cedri; p.119 top Larrain-Magnum; bottom Larrain-Magnum; p.120 top Sioen-Cedri; bottom Gerster-Rapho; p.121 Serraillier-Rapho; p.122 top Sioen-Cedri; bottom A. Hutchison Lby; p.123 Sioen-Cedri; p.124 Depardon-Magnum; p.125 Depardon-Magnum; p.126 E. Guillou; p.127 M. Bruggmann; p.128 Sioen-Cedri; p.129 Sioen-Cedri; p.130 top

Sioen-Cedri; bottom S. Held; p.131 Sioen-Cedri; p.132 Sioen-Cedri; p.133 Sioen-Cedri; p.134 Sioen-Cedri; p.135 A. Reffet; p.136 A. Reffet; p.137 left A.Reffet; right S. Held; p.138 Sioen-Cedri; p.139 Regior-Explorer; p.140 A.Reffet; p.141 top Sioen-Cedri; bottom A. Reffet; p.142 A. Reffet; p.143 Duchêne-Diaf; p.144 left Wright-A. Hutchison Lby; right Wright-A. Hutchison Lby; p. 145 Sioen-Cedri; p.146 Sioen-Cedri; p.146/147 Dumas-Fotogram; p.147 Sioen-Cedri; p.148 Sioen-Cedri

Cover pictures:
Top: Jerry Alexander-Tony Stone Worldwide
Bottom: South American Pictures